HENRY MILLER

HENRY MILLER

The Paris Years

BY BRASSAÏ

Translated from the French by Timothy Bent

With Photographs by the Author

ARCADE PUBLISHING • NEW YORK

FIRST ENGLISH-LANGUAGE EDITION

Originally published in France under the title *Henry Miller, grandeur nature*

Excerpts from *Henry Miller's Hamlet Letters*, edited by Michael Hargraves, copyright © 1988 by Capra Press, reprinted by permission of Capra Press, Santa Barbara, CA.

Excerpts from *The Durrell-Miller Letters 1935-1980*, copyright © 1963 by Laurence Durrell and Henry Miller, *Remember to Remember*, copyright © 1961 by Henry Miller, and *Wisdom of the Heart*, copyright © 1960 by Henry Miller, reprinted by permission of New Directions Publishing Corporation.

Library of Congress Cataloging-in-Publication Data

Brassaï, 1899–1984
    [Henry Miller, grandeur nature. English]
    Henry Miller, the Paris years / Brassaï ; translated from the French by Timothy Bent. — 1st English language ed.
       p.   cm.
    ISBN 1-55970-287-7 (hc)
    ISBN 1-55970-347-4 (pb)
      1. Miller, Henry, 1891–1980 — Homes and haunts — France — Paris.   2. Paris (France) — Intellectual life — 20th century.   3. Americans — France — Paris — History — 20th century.   4. Authors, American — 20th century — Biography.   5. Brassaï, 1899–1984 — Friends and associates. I. Title.
PS3525.I5454Z65713   1995
818'.5209 — dc20   94–39261
[B]

Published in the United States by Arcade Publishing, Inc., New York

Distributed by Little, Brown and Company

10 9 8 7 6 5 4 3 2 1

Designed by API

Maps by Jeffrey L. Ward

BP

PRINTED IN THE UNITED STATES OF AMERICA

To Raymond Queneau

Contents

TRANSLATOR'S NOTE

Brassaï's portrait of Henry Miller's Paris years ranges freely among, and extracts generously from, Miller's works. With the exception of several letters Miller sent him, Brassaï has based his citations on translations. Every attempt has been made to locate and use the original—though indications weren't always clear—and a bibliography at the end of the book lists the editions of works employed herein. Sources for some citations, such as those taken from correspondence between Miller and Frank Dobo or from transcripts of conversations between Dobo and Brassaï, were not traceable. Quotations from works originally written in French have been translated for this volume; citations refer to the original versions used by Brassaï.

HENRY MILLER

I

On the Terrace at the Dôme

"How does my memory of this compare with yours? I seem to see you standing in the gutter at the Dôme, *à l'angle de la rue Delambre et Blvd Montparnasse* . . . You had a newspaper in your hand. You told us you had begun to practice photography. It may have been the yĕar 1931. The spot where you stood I see so vividly that I could draw a circle around it." In a letter to me, this was how Henry Miller recalled our first meeting. "It's strange," he told me, "but with most people we remember neither where nor under what circumstances we met. But I remember the first time you and I met as if it were yesterday."

My memory doesn't quite compare with his. My memory of the first time Henry and I met was that it took place in December 1930, shortly after he had arrived in France. My friend the painter Louis Tihanyi introduced us. Louis was sort of the Dôme's PR man — everyone recognized his olive green corduroy overcoat, worn to a shine, his wide-brimmed gray felt hat, his monocle, his fleshy lower lip. He was the

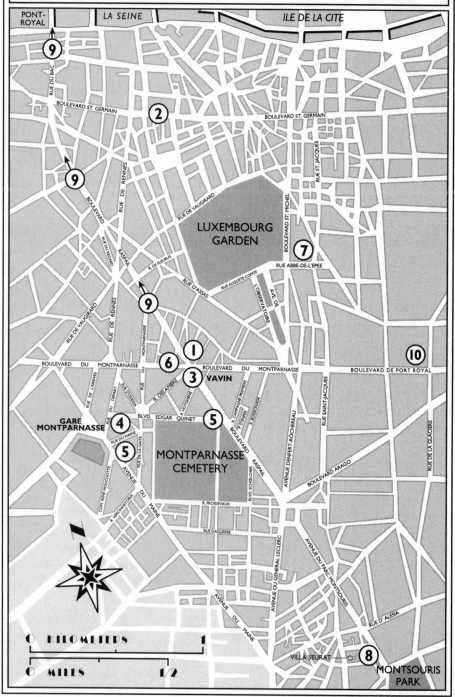

1 "'I seem to see you standing in the gutter at the Dôme, *à l'angle de la rue Delambre et Blvd Montparnasse. . .* You had a newspaper in your hand. You told us you had begun to practice photography'" (letter from HM to Brassaï).

2 "Each time he passed by the statue of Etienne Dolet—Rabelais's printer and the publisher of *Pantagruel*—on Boulevard Saint-Germain, Miller reflected on the woes that might befall Jack Kahane. Dolet was hanged and burned for spreading subversive ideas."

3 "Somehow, over the years, the very name Montparnasse had acquired power, and for a very long time, particularly around the mouth of the Métro stop at Vavin, one could still feel the mood of festivity—in pure Belle Époque fashion—to which all of Paris had once abandoned itself. In a world turned sour, even a bourgeoisie and a petite-bourgeoisie in search of pleasure and joy were drawn to this place of euphoria, liberty, and nonconformity, this place that became for a time Henry Miller's real home."

4/5 "Perlès . . . took Miller home to share his room at the Central Hôtel on Rue du Maine on the very day of Miller's arrival. Long before Perlès was awake, Miller would have ventured into the wonderful chaos of the street market on Edgar-Quinet, or have walked through the marvelous passageways of pterocaryas that were so dear to that other exile Rousseau—who drew inspiration from them to write about his virgin forests—and then have made his way along the walls of the Montparnasse cemetery, where Baudelaire lay buried. Some mornings he would wander down Rue de la Gaîté, which was a kind of Broadway in miniature, with its bars, moviehouses, and a popular music hall called the Bobino."

6 "Broke and weary, we would often sit at the Dôme or the Rotonde, order a café crème and a sandwich, then wait for deliverance: that friend who would happen by and cover the tab for you."

7 "He credited the French with nearly always choosing exactly the right place to put these strange and delicate structures, lit from within like a lantern. He loved the sound of water running over the tile, as if over the floor of a cave. Miller's particular favorite was the urinal right in front of the home for deaf-mutes on the corner of Rue Saint-Jacques and Rue Abbé-de-l'Epée."

8 "Anaïs wanted Henry to move back to Paris, and the idea of his living in the Villa Seurat had long preoccupied her. That summer she visited this elegant little cul-de-sac located in the 14th arrondissement, between Montparnasse and Montsouris Park and consisting of twenty small art-deco houses—each one painted a different color—and rented an apartment for Henry."

9 "To get [to American Express] from Montparnasse, you descended Boulevard Raspail, crossed the Seine at Pont-Royal, traversed the Tuileries to Avenue de l'Opéra, then up to Rue Scribe. By taxi, car, subway, bus, carriage, and most often on foot, every American who has ever lived in Paris has trod this path of hope and dreams."

10 "At the time I was trying to finish *Paris by Night*, my first book of photography and a study of Paris lowlife. Miller was insatiably curious about the project, and often came to see me at the Hôtel des Terrasses, which was located on Rue de la Glacière in the 13th arrondissement. For hour after hour he pored over my nightly harvest of photographs, which were stretched out across the bed."

spitting image of Alphonse XIII — minus the pencil mustache. Every night, table by table, Louis worked the crowded Dôme terrace, which, beneath the luminous green shade of the trees on the boulevard, was always festive, as if every day were Bastille. Although deaf, and very nearly dumb as well, Louis was the best-informed man in Montparnasse. He knew not only every single one of the regulars, but the measure and worth of each newcomer.

"I want you to meet Henry Miller, an American writer," he announced in his abrupt, guttural voice, which somehow always managed to make itself heard over the hum of conversations and the noise from the street.

And there was Henry Miller. I will never forget the first sight of his rosy face emerging from a rumpled raincoat: the pouting, full lower lip, eyes the color of the sea. His eyes were like those of a sailor skilled at scanning the horizons through the spray. They always conveyed calmness and serenity, those eyes, and even though their expression seemed as guileless and attentive as a dog's, they lay in ambush behind large tortoiseshell glasses. When we met they were scrutinizing me with curiosity. When he took off his crumpled gray hat, the dome of his bald skull, haloed by silvery hair, reflected the café's neon lights. He was slender and gnarled, and without so much as one ounce of excess body fat. He reminded me of an ascetic, a mandarin, a Tibetan holy man. Had some makeup artist fit him with a mustache, long gray hair, and a patriarchal beard, Miller, with his crinkled, Asiatic eyes, his strong nose and flared, aristocratic nostrils, would have looked exactly like Leo Tolstoy. I will never forget the first time that I heard his sonorous bass voice — warm and virile, punctuated by "yesses" and "hmms," and accompanied by a deep, gentle rumble of pleasure.

June, Henry's wife — who would be the Mona and the

4

Mara in his books — had been to Paris before him. She'd run away there in 1927 with her Russian friend, leaving Henry behind to mope all by himself in their basement apartment in New York. June had taken up residence in the Princesse Hôtel, located on the Left Bank near Saint-Germain-des-Prés. When she returned to New York later that same year, loaded down with stories and gifts, Henry thought she looked more beautiful than ever. Her return blotted out the whole tragedy of her betrayal, just as the title of the work he had planned to write about it all changed from *Crucifixion* to *The Rosy Crucifixion*. Henry was dying to know all about Paris, and bombarded her with questions. Had she seen Picasso? Matisse? She replied that she hadn't. She had, however, made the acquaintance of Zadkin, Marcel Duchamp, Edgar Varèse, Michonze, Tihanyi, and other artists of whose names Miller had not yet heard, although later they were to become his friends. In 1928, having managed to scrape together enough money to do so, June returned to France, and this time she took Henry. They visited nearly every European country and spent a full year in Paris.

Tihanyi met Henry during this first trip, and immediately realized when he saw him again in 1930, during the second trip, that he was not one of those typical rich Americans, ready to buy one of your paintings or treat you to a good dinner, but — a somewhat rare thing in Paris in those days — a penniless Yankee with neither name, reputation, nor fixed abode. The Paris police would have been within their rights to arrest Miller for vagrancy and haul him down to the station. The man's entire fortune consisted of a toothbrush, a razor, a notebook, a pen, a raincoat, and a Mexican cane that he had brought over with him. "I have only physical, biological problems," he tells his friend Michael Fraenkel in one of their *Hamlet* letters. Fraenkel himself led a life of ease and wanted to talk philosophy with

Henry. "When I say I am hungry," writes Henry, "you talk about my soul or about my lack of loyalty. Whereas all I ask is a little food, *real* food." Almost forty, life's midpoint, Miller often had no idea where his next meal was coming from, or whether he would have a roof over his head that night. Yet he betrayed absolutely no anxiety about this. Indeed, he was serene, almost angelic, about his precarious existence. "I have no money, no resources, no hopes," he writes at the beginning of *Tropic of Cancer.* "I am the happiest man alive." He would tell people that all the time. Then laugh his sonorous laugh.

In *Interviews* [*Entretiens*], André Breton recounted that before the publication of the *First Surrealist Manifesto,* he and his friends Aragon, Roger Vitrac, and Max Morise, among others, had tried to follow Rimbaud's famous injunction to "drop everything and hit the road," but that this hadn't turned out to be so easy. To become a bum, a pilgrim, to go shuffling off in your slippers without either money or anything in the stomach? This had proved too much for these young men of privilege and they failed at vagabondage. Miller, on the other hand, succeeded. He cleansed his soul by roaming the streets of Paris without a single sou in his pocket. "I was born in the street," he liked to tell people. What was life for if not for wandering through? And indeed his idol was none other than Rimbaud, about whose wanderings he wrote in *The Time of the Assassins,* "In all these flights and sallies he is always without money, always walking, and walking usually on an empty stomach." In later years Henry often recalled the euphoria of his days *en marge,* on the fringes, fraught though they were with uncertainty and even misery. He was happy.

He had his reasons for feeling happy. Crossing the Atlantic, leaving behind New York with its skyscrapers, and June with all her turbulent passions, had been an act of liberation for Henry. In Paris, and particularly in that special, otherworldly place that Montparnasse still was in the thirties, he could breathe deep the air of freedom. He could have cared less that he had no bed, no food, no tobacco. *Bagatelle!* He was inspired. He had escaped the slave drivers and outrun the dogs they'd set on him. In Paris he was like a man released from prison, rubbing his eyes and pinching himself — was all this real?

I never truly understood the reasons for Henry's need to escape from America until later, after I had spent some time there myself. In Europe, poverty was purely a matter of bad luck; in the United States it was a sign of moral defect, a badge of shame that society could not pardon. It reminds me of the difference between the Guermantes family and the Combray bourgeoisie in Proust's work. Like Brahmins, the bourgeoisie wants to classify everyone according to income, while the Guermanteses, who attach no significance whatever to fortune, realize that although poverty is disagreeable, it is not a mark of dishonor. Miller had finally been unable to stomach the feeling of shame any longer — that was what he had had to escape from. Madness or suicide were the alternatives. "I have walked the streets in many countries of the world," he says in *Tropic of Capricorn*, "but nowhere have I felt so degraded and humiliated as in America." In France, his brow unfurrowed and he became expansive. His whole being radiated irrepressible optimism.

★   ★   ★

Paris had changed between 1928 and 1930, between Miller's first trip and his second. Men's hats — especially the derbies, the *melons*, of yore — had nearly disappeared, as had gaiters, starched collars, trams and tramways, gaslights, and horses (except those white Percherons that still pulled the carts carrying ice and Jaffa oranges). As for women, liberated from their corsets by Paul Poiret and Coco Chanel, they had begun to adopt a masculine look, and took to wearing crumpled hats, doing their hair *à la coup de vent*, and dressing in comfortable skirts *à la garçonne*.

Black Thursday — October 24, 1929 — had rocked the world. During a time of seeming prosperity, the New York stock market had suddenly been gripped by panic and madness. The Wall Street crash plunged America into the worst crisis of its existence, opening a yawning gulf into which some fifteen billion dollars disappeared without a trace. The effects of that fateful day were soon felt around the world. Today we see that it stands as the midpoint between two world wars. At the time it was clear only that it signaled an end to carefree abundance — those years of easy money that had been the making of fashion, art galleries, travel bureaus, and floozies.

The full impact of the crisis reached France nearly at about the moment Miller did. He had timed his second arrival to coincide perfectly with the end of the *années folles* — that crazy ten-year period between the Armistice and the Crash — and the beginning of a lean age of bankruptcy, misery, unemployment. Successful artists had to sell off their *hôtels particuliers* in order to eat; less successful ones joined the same soup lines as the rest of the population. And as for the American artists (always recognizable because of the checkered shirts they wore), of which a colony had thrived in Paris, the Depression forced them home in droves. Their families were more or less financially ruined, and with their wallets emptied of dollars they returned sadly across the Atlantic. The city gradually lost its foreign artists while the crisis steadily worsened: thirty million people around the world had lost their jobs. In Germany alone the unemployment figure reached four million. Hitler received ten million votes in the German elections of 1931; he got fourteen million two years later, and became chancellor. France abandoned the Rhineland. Fearing a German attack, the government ordered the construction of the Maginot Line. Hope, insouciance, and cheer were replaced by worry, anxiety, and bleakness.

But if there was a place where some of life's sweetness lingered still, it was most certainly Montparnasse, which for the most part had been miraculously spared the *mal du siècle*. Why this charmless and unpicturesque corner of Paris, surrounded by wealthy apartment buildings altogether lacking in character, had become a center of artistic life — sealed off from all the cultural and even the social revolutions raging around it — remains a mystery. Somehow, over the years, the very name Montparnasse had acquired power, and for a very long time, particularly around the mouth of the Métro stop at Vavin, one could still feel the mood of festivity — in pure Belle Epoque fashion — to which all of Paris had once abandoned itself. In a world turned sour, even a bourgeoisie and a petite-bourgeoisie in search of pleasure and joy were drawn to this place of euphoria, liberty, and nonconformity, this place that became for a time Henry Miller's real home.

His first friend in France was Alfred Perlès, whom he had met in Montparnasse in 1928. Two years later, penniless, he found Perlès sitting at the same table at the Dôme. "The ass was out of my breeches and my tongue was hanging out," Miller recalled in a circular he wrote in 1935 to raise money for Perlès, who had lost his job when the *Chicago Herald Tribune* abruptly ceased operations the year before. The circular bears the somewhat ridiculous-sounding title "What Are You Going to Do About Alf?" The strong bond that formed between them undoubtedly had to do with their German ancestry. Miller's background was German through and through. He had spoken German at home before he started school. His neighborhood of Brooklyn was called "Little Germany." "That damned German music, so melancholy, so sentimental," he recalls in *Tropic of Cancer.* "We were brought up on Schumann and Hugo Wolf and sauerkraut and kümmel and potato dumplings." And the Viennese Perlès, as sentimental as the music his city produced, connected with the *gemütlich* spirit of Miller's youth.

"He brought me food and cigarettes," wrote Henry in "What Are You Going to do About Alf?" "He left money for me on the mantelpiece, in his delicate way. He found me a job. He sang and danced for me when my spirits lagged. He taught me French — the little I know. In brief, he put me on my feet again." Perlès (whom Miller would call "Fred," "Alf," "Joe," "Joey," and, in *Tropic of Cancer,* "Carl") took Miller home to share his room at the Central Hôtel on Rue du Maine on the very day of Miller's arrival. The windows on the upper floors looked down on a charming little square with benches, a few linden trees, and gas lamps. Perlès worked at the *Chicago Herald Tribune* at night, sometimes returning very late and sleeping until noon. Miller was a morning person, out and about early, doing reconnaissance on his new turf. Long before Perlès was awake, Miller would have ventured into the wonderful chaos of the street market on Edgar-Quinet, or have walked through the marvelous passageways of pterocaryas that were so dear to Henri Rousseau — who drew inspiration from them to paint his virgin forests — and then have made his way along the walls of the Montparnasse cemetery, where Baudelaire lay buried. Some mornings he would wander down Rue de la Gaîté, which was a kind of Broadway in miniature, with its bars, moviehouses, and a popular music hall called the Bobino.

Fred was already a seasoned Parisian by the time of my own arrival in France in 1924, the year I met him. He had lived in Paris since 1920. He never talked about his past. I learned, little by little, that he had lived in Yugoslavia, Prague, Berlin, Amsterdam, Copenhagen, Italy, even Morocco. There is a photograph showing him perched on a rock in Africa and sporting a thick beard. I also learned that he had lived through some tough times. He had a genius for languages. He had written several novels in German, though no one knew anything about them, and was then in the process of writing two more in French: *Sentiments limitrophes* and *Quatuor en ré mineur* [*Feelings from the Front*, and *Quartet in D Minor*]. Perlès also spoke and wrote English extremely well, which was why he had been hired as an editor at the *Tribune*, and would even occasionally correct Miller's somewhat more casual usage. A character from Fred's novel *Quartet in D Minor*, which Henry particularly admired, and quoted in his essay "Remember to Remember," provides a self-portrait:

> I am timid and of uneven temperament, *Himmelhoch jauchzend, zu Tode betrübt* ['shouting with joy, and mortally depressed']. Sudden feelings of melancholy and alarming explosions of joy alternate in me, with absolutely no transition. If I sometimes seem cynical it is because of my timidity and because I fear ridicule. I am always ready to dissolve into tears and that is why I feel the need to subvert my noblest sentiments. A form of masochism, doubtless.

The friendship between Fred and Henry — Henry termed it an "intimate association" — soon took the form of a symbiotic relationship whose chief purpose was to ensure mutual survival, and to facilitate their three principal preoccupations: eating, having sex, and writing. Until 1934, when the *Tribune* closed down, Fred had a fixed salary, but it was barely enough to live on. By the time payday rolled around, after he had stuffed himself and paid off his back rent, he had almost nothing left. Fred and Henry were therefore forced to use their wits to find money, or to pray for a "windfall." Those windfalls fell, with some frequency, generally in the form of wealthy American tourists (especially women) visiting Montparnasse with plenty of money.

Miller's brand of nihilism fit in perfectly with Perlès's form of cynicism, and with his beyond-good-and-evil sort of attitude. They were the best of friends, lusty co-conspirators, and shared everything: a bed, a bowl of porridge at the Coupole, a plate of fried potatoes cooked up on an alcohol-fueled hotplate, money, wine, cigarettes, even women. "If you were a friend he would share his women with you, in the same way that he would share his last crust of bread," Miller wrote in "Remember to Remember." "Some people found this hard to forgive in him, this ability to share everything. He expected others to act the same way, of course. If they refused he was ruthless." Henry and Fred were like Siamese twins. They lied for each other, cheated for each other, stole for each other. They even put each other's name to a short story or essay after it had been rejected under their own. Thus, several pieces of Miller's work appear under Alfred Perlès's name in the *Chicago Herald Tribune* — among them, "Rue Lourmel in the Fog" (April 1932) and "Paris in C Minor" (March 3, 1933). The two friends also palmed off publishers on each other. Henry once told me a story about that:

> One editor, Maurice Dekobra's — which is not a recommendation — used to visit Anaïs Nin at Louveciennes. One day he asked if he could publish something of mine: "My novel isn't finished," I replied, "but I have a friend who's a writer, a real genius . . . He's just finished an extraordinary novel . . . You should contact him, and

maybe he'd be willing to allow you to publish something of his . . ." Of course I was thinking of Fred, who was trying in vain to find a publisher for *Feelings from the Front*. Miracle! The editor published his novel. Another editor, very devout, an author himself of a very Christian and tearful book in favor of peace, was looking for an English translator and contacted Fred. Fred urged him to get in touch with me — blasphemous, immoral, pornographic — expounding the purity of my soul and my virtues . . . And by some miracle I got the job. He suggested 1,000 francs, and I asked for 5, which is what he paid me.

There was something remarkable about the friendship between these two. Physically, they were complete opposites. Henry was a tower of energy and Fred was somewhat puny. Fred worshiped Miller, telling him over and over that he was a genius. Then he would add, "And you're also a pimp!" "Well, you're a rat," Miller would tease back, proceeding to call him a rogue, a rascal, and a scoundrel. But from his lips these weren't insults. Miller put Fred in that class of libertines and freethinkers who sneered at the law, social conventions, and creature comforts, and admired him all the more for it. Fred boasted that he was a poltroon, a coward, an ingrate, and a traitor (though of course his boasting often revealed just how good-hearted and courageous he was). Miller would tell people that Fred could lie as easily as tell the truth: "He's as slippery as an eel."

Fred was indeed so good at impersonations that you sometimes didn't know which one was the real Fred. He could be a Yankee straight-talker, a gentleman of reserve and dignity, a *gemütlich* Viennese charmer, a doddering old Frenchman. He had only three possessions, though they were of very high quality: a tweed suit that he wore everywhere, made by a good English tailor near the

Opéra, a dusty Remington rifle, and an enormous, solid gold Parker pen.

Fred's uncanny ability to imitate others never failed him except when he tried to imitate Miller's muscular prose. It was clear that his own writing, delicate and sentimental, was no match for his friend's. Henry, for his part, would have nothing to do with what he saw as the lachrymose pessimism in Fred's writing. Yet despite their differences (perhaps because of them), and despite all the difficulties entailed in living and surviving in Paris during those grim years, the Miller-Perlès duo was a happy one. Life was not passing them by. "During all these years of intimate association," recalls Henry in "Remember to Remember," "we were always fully conscious of the fact that we were enjoying life to the hilt. We knew there could not be anything better than what we were experiencing every day of our lives."

In the Middle Ages, great lords would surround themselves with jesters, on whom they counted to create a mood of wit and fun. Miller, who thought seriousness a serious defect and a true character flaw, a disease that raged among intellectuals especially, found in Fred the preordained embodiment of his own marvelous sense of buffoonery. Fred was a born clown. His pink, oval face, which, when he was caught up in a laughing fit, could turn as bright red as a beet, was hilariously rubbery. He could make the most outlandish expressions with it. Fred was himself well aware of this, and reveled in his gifts — and in the infectious, irrepressible volleys of howling laughter that it set off. Seconds after we met, I remember, he was seized by contortions of laughter. "I don't seem to recall a single day in which we did not laugh heartily, often until the tears came to our eyes."

Perlès's laughter contained a whole philosophy of its own, as we might guess from that novelistic self-portrait in which he tells the reader that he felt "the need to subvert my noblest sentiments." He taught Miller to glory in the present, to take life lightly, and to laugh at everything and everyone. This side-splitting laughter, which respected, says Miller, neither God nor toilet paper, could turn the most solemn declarations and the most venerable of institutions into instant objects of ridicule. It was the laugh of a playful dolphin, a "celestial porpoise."

★　　★　　★

In 1953, after they hadn't seen each other in fifteen years or so, Henry met Fred in Barcelona. The very minute he saw Fred's ear-to-ear grin, he burst out laughing. And the ringing laughter — "from the heart and from the belly" — continued unabated until they parted forty-eight hours later. So contagious was it that Eve, Miller's wife at the time, and Joseph and Caroline Delteil, who were with them, couldn't help but join in. It was only when they were on the verge of parting that Henry and Fred's laughter quieted. "I haven't stopped laughing, even in my sleep," Miller wrote Perlès. "I laughed and we all laughed across Spain when you came up." Henry was delirious at finding Fred again, if only for a few hours. Wonderful memories of their "golden days" and "precious carefreeness" came rushing back to him. Fred's irrepressible laughter and devil-may-care ways had taught him more than all the books of wisdom he had devoured.

II

Paris in 1930

During the 1928 trip with June, Miller had looked at Paris through the eyes of a Yankee tourist: blasé and totally uninterested in historical sites, monuments, or any other remnants of the past. June had told Henry that Paris would be his kind of place. "It's where you belong!" she'd exclaimed. "You'll find there what you can't find here." The first time around, however, Paris did not sweep him off his feet. Actually, he thought that the other European cities they'd visited — Budapest, Prague, Vienna — were far more seductive. His stay in Paris left him feeling indifferent, and the city didn't figure as the place to which he wanted to return; Madrid had that honor. When he got to Paris the second time, however, he didn't have the money to go farther. All he had when he got on the boat was ten dollars, which his childhood friend Emil Schnellock had lent him at the last minute.

At the moment of his departure for Paris, Miller described himself as "An expatriate from Brooklyn, a francophile, a vagabond, a writer at the beginning of his career, naive, enthusiastic, absorbent as a sponge, interested in everything and seemingly rudderless" (*A Devil in Paradise*). This time, Paris worked miracles. "Perhaps America had nothing to do with it, but the fact remains that I did not open my eyes wide and full and clear until I struck Paris" (*Tropic of Capricorn*).

Marcel, Proust's protagonist, having despaired for the whole length of the narrative about being a failed writer, suddenly discovers, at the end of *Time Recovered*, that by a deus ex machina he has become the celebrated author of *Remembrance of Things Past*. So too Miller, having sketched out and then abandoned thousands of projects for some twenty years, suddenly found his literary way in Paris. Proust was, of course, not "Marcel"; he was far from being that talentless man tortured by feelings of worthlessness. The real Marcel was acutely aware of his gifts. What Miller needed, on the other hand, was a miracle.

★   ★   ★

"What trouble one goes through before *coming back to one-self*," Jules Renard used to say. By the time he settled in Paris, Miller had been looking for his true writing self for some twenty years. The desire to be a real writer haunted him like a ghost. "It was time to decide what I was going to write. However, the very minute I tried to find a subject, my brain stopped working and all I could see was empty space." That's not Miller, that's "Marcel" in *Swann's Way*, yet their distress seems interchangeable. Miller used nearly the same words to describe his own fear that he didn't have what it takes to be a writer. As soon as they started to write, Marcel and Henry were paralyzed by the "virgin white page, devoid of any writing." *L'Ennui* made the pen drop from both men's hands, and they wept from frustration: "Once again I felt my intellectual nothingness and that I was not born for writing," writes Marcel in *Within a Budding Grove*. Miller and Marcel were both plagued by the doubt that perhaps they should abandon their literary ambitions. Before them lay the void, and curse, of the "virgin white page."

Yet, during their long stints in Purgatory, Miller and Marcel also experienced brief, euphoric flashes of illumination that, for brief moments, would soothe their fears of impotency. Marcel could feel "irrational pleasure" at the sight of a roof, the play of sunlight, or a young girl's face, because the pleasure brought with it the prophetic assurance that he would make it as a writer. A thought that hadn't been there the moment before had suddenly burst into language. When he succeeded in describing those bells of Martinville — and by so doing, ridding himself of them — he felt such drunken joy that he starting singing at the top of his lungs.

Only on paper could Henry and Marcel confide their secrets. In *Sexus*, rereading a passage from one of his books, a passage about walking as a child "across sunlit fields" while holding his mother's hand, Miller thought it so good that "tears came to my eyes." Again in *Sexus*, he describes one of those "odd moments of inspiration," or "attacks," a moment of perception so acute that he knows that something has changed: "I realized that a new element was manifesting itself, one which had portentous significance. This element was awareness." These moments of illumination drew Miller and Marcel to the borders of language, to the frontiers of the promised land.

Henry never ceased trying to understand the reasons behind the Paris "miracle." His long dry spells he blamed on the sterility of America, where what was missing for any writer was an explicit faith in the writing profession. In America he had mistakenly wanted to become a "man of letters," a classic novelist of the sort who creates characters and plots and is obedient to narrative forms. He dreamed of Thomas Mann's fame the way Marcel dreamed of Bergotte's. Miller had lost his originality under the spell of other writers. Lawrence Durrell, who had the chance to read some of Henry's early works, told me that finding the traces of the author of the *Tropics* in them was impossible. Miller himself acknowledged that everything he wrote before he got to Paris had been inspired by someone else. In Paris he found his own voice.

For this liberating Paris to be revealed to him, Miller needed to experience it not as a tourist, but as a vagrant. He needed to undergo a trial that was both difficult and enriching — and avoided by so many writers: living *en marge*. Blaise Cendrars, who had himself undergone a trial like it in New York ("a poor fugitive in the mean streets of a large foreign city"), understood perfectly how much Henry owed to his down-and-out period. In an essay on Miller entitled "Unto Us An American Writer Is Born," published in the magazine *Orbe*, Cendrars wrote: "Discovering Paris, breathing Paris, devouring Paris, he swallowed furiously, and ate it, then he wanted to vomit in it and piss against it, adore it and curse it until he felt that he was part of the extraordinary people in the streets of this great city, until Paris had gotten under his skin and he knew that from that day forward he could never live anywhere else." As Miller himself recalled in an interview with Georges Belmont in 1970 about the second trip to Paris: "There had to be a second time, a time when I was totally broke, desperate, and living like a vagrant in the streets to start to see and to live the real Paris. I was discovering it at the same time that I was discovering myself." Henry would often say that what he found in France was nothing less than the "new will to live."

★   ★   ★

To a man looking with fresh eyes, everything about Paris fascinates. Miller wanted to see everything, hear everything, understand everything. In wasteful, unholy New York, a city simultaneously rotting and renewing, everything is newly renovated, just built, or under construction. What Miller was delighted to find in Paris was an economizing spirit, signs of stinginess, a maniacal need to conserve even the most ramshackle. In the small, run-down hotels, decrepit with age — of which Henry was to know some two or three dozen — most bearing grandiloquent names such as Hotel of the Future, Hotel of Progress, Hotel Splendid, Modern Hotel, Hotel of the Twentieth Century, and so on, the cult of the discarded, the threadbare, the frayed, and the outdated completely disarmed him. The appearance of luxury, in all its ricketiness, could be found everywhere — in the beds, bidets, armchairs, and armoires. Faded carpets were sewn together to cover the sagging, teetering steps in the stairways, the remnants held together by metallic strips nailed to each step. (These strips were also supposed to increase bounce.) Henry noted that these eyesores usually extended no farther than the first or second floor. The rugs in the rooms, having lost most of their nap, were the color of a mole suffering from a skin affliction. Most of the easy chairs required the assistance of wires, ropes, and leather straps to keep from collapsing. A bare light bulb suspended in the middle of the room provided only slightly more illumination than a candle. The result was immediate eyestrain. Turn on the faucet, and what you got was a gurgling that shook the whole floor. This same chaos was unleashed every time your neighbor next door, or above, or below, took a bath or flushed the toilet.

Before he went to Paris this second time, Miller had familiarized himself with its geography. Emil Schnellock — "Ulric" in his narratives — had taken him around the City of Light by means of a map, pointing out the location of every museum, cemetery, train station, whorehouse, and *bal musette*. And in 1928, Henry and June had of course already explored Paris's streets and *grands boulevards*. They had walked up and down the Champs Elysées. On that first trip, Henry's ability to communicate with the natives had been limited to stammering, "*A votre service, Madame!*" "*Merci, Monsieur!*" "*Au revoir, Monsieur!*" and "*S'il vous plaît, Mademoiselle!*" He had dreamed of chestnut trees in bloom, sidewalk cafés, and caped policemen patrolling the night, only to be disappointed. The second trip revealed the reality behind these clichés, and Henry was spellbound.

He was impressed by how many bookstores there were, and how many art galleries (still rare in the United States in those days). He was also surprised by how understated French books looked. They seemed to emphasize content rather than packaging, and indeed the most extraordinary books might be found behind the most unassuming covers. And there were so many streets named for artists and writers! Rue Balzac, Avenue Victor-Hugo, Rue Lamartine, Rue Racine, and on and on. He was charmed by all those bookstalls along the Seine. He concluded that in Paris, art and literature — the spiritual dimension of humanity — were recognized, admired, and even valued. The very air was saturated with them.

Miller was also delighted to discover the parks, the squares, the trees — those sycamores and chestnuts lining the avenues, the beeches along the Seine, the paulownias with their perfumed purple flowers, in the Place D'Italie, the pterocaryas on Boulevard Edgar-Quinet. Aside from Central Park and some of the waterfronts, New York, in sharp contrast, had given itself over to cement and asphalt, and was, as he writes in *Tropic of Cancer*, "cold, glittering, malign."

In the Paris of 1930 (which was a rather provincial city compared to New York) Miller re-found something of his fin-de-siècle youth, which had always had more in common with Europe than with America. Whenever I mentioned the Belle Epoque, or those famous cafés once frequented by artists, Miller would tell me how much he regretted not having seen the prewar Paris, not having known Apollinaire, Max Jacob, Picasso, and Toulouse-Lautrec, not having haunted Montparnasse in its heyday. I once told him that when I was five, in 1904, I had spent a year in Paris, and pushed a little sailboat around the pool in the Luxembourg Gardens. He was immediately envious of my memory. "You knew the Paris of Marcel Proust! You saw the procession of vehicles in the Bois de Boulogne! You sauntered down the *grands boulevards!* You saw Paris at the imperial height of the Madeleine-Bastille horse-drawn omnibus!"

Of all his new discoveries, Henry was most delighted by those oases of peace and idleness that can be found in all Latin countries, and which abound in Paris: sidewalk cafés. For the simple price of a cup of coffee or a beer, you could write, talk, listen to conversations, meet people, daydream, people-watch, and let the world go by. This was a form of recreation almost unknown to anyone living in America at the time, and what truly amazed Henry was that it all cost so little. We sometimes spent entire days in the cafés. Broke and weary, we would often sit at the Dôme or the Rotonde, order a *café crème* and a sandwich, then wait for deliverance: that friend who would happen by and cover the tab for you. If you had to wait for more than a few hours, you started to worry. Henry was often forced to resort to this technique, which he likened to fishing. He was used to it. Back in New York, he'd sometimes had to wait around in a bar all night before he caught someone with the money to unhook him.

Miller was also amazed by the bistros, the *zincs* (café countertops), the charcoal, and those little masterpieces of popular art, lovingly hand-drawn and displayed daily: the restaurant menus. For a while he even collected them. They spoke not only to his eyes, but to his nostrils and to his "innards." The names of the dishes, the cheeses, and especially the wines exerted an almost magical power over him. He would repeat them over and over like a prayer or an incantation: Montrachet, Clos-Vougeot, Vosne-Romanée, Nuits-Saint-Georges, Meursault, Gevrey-Chamtertin, Château-Yquem, Haut-Brion, Mouton-Rothschild. When he lived at the Villa Seurat, Miller religiously conserved the empty relics of French viticulture and put them next to his black desk. Every so often he would pick one up, reread the label, and be moved again. He adored the modest bistros as much as he did the starred restaurants, the ordinary *pinards* as much as the grand *crus*. Eating and drinking were at the core of French life, of French *savoir-vivre*. He thought that descriptions of feasts and drinking deserved an anthology all their own. As did the women who served him. These ladies from Provence, Picardy, Bourgogne, Dordogne — most certainly underrated and less stylish than their New York counterparts — embodied, in Miller's eyes, all the prestige of their respective provinces in the same way that the prostitutes did.

From eating and drinking, we proceed to the *déboire* stage and into the Parisian urinals. Before he came to Paris, Miller knew of these *vespasiennes* from books and hearsay, and they were subjects of nostalgia and enthusiasm for him even before he'd had a chance to experience them himself.

He credited the French with nearly always choosing exactly the right place to put these strange and delicate structures, lit from within like a lantern. He loved the sound of water running over the tile, as if over the floor of a cave. Miller's particular favorite was the urinal right in front of the home for deaf-mutes on the corner of Rue Saint-Jacques and Rue Abbé-de-l'Epée.

Proust also paid homage to the water closet, particularly to the one that he used to frequent on the Champs Elysées — a small pavilion trellised in green from the fresh odors of the enclosure — and to the one he locked himself in at Combray. While we're on the subject, I would like to note that the seatless toilets, the ones consisting simply of a hole in the floor and two platforms for the feet (feet the size of an abominable snowman's) — the so-called "Turkish toilets" that have provoked such feelings of dread and disgust in foreigners — won over the sympathy of Henry Miller. He sang their praises, heartily concurring with the doctors that as regards this task the crouched position is more hygienic than the sitting position. Miller had a certain weakness for those enclosures in which, once a day at least, "one is alone with oneself," and where, at times, one could spend a "moment of bliss," as he writes in his essay "Reading in the Toilet." He found the same spirit of simplicity in the Turkish toilets that he had in the softcover books, the triumph of efficiency over show.

Another thing that struck Miller was the word *défense*. It seemed to be everywhere he looked — on walls, on the sides of churches and buildings, on doors, lawns, stairways: *Défense d'afficher, Défense d'uriner, Défense d'entrer, Défense de fumer, Défense de toucher aux objets*. [Post No Bills, No Urinating, No Entry, No Smoking, No Touching.] *Défense* cast its long shadow everywhere. In America, generally speaking, there were no walls, gates, or barbed wires between properties. Because there was no closed door — not even a bank president's — that you couldn't walk through, no lawn that you couldn't tread on, even in the most beautiful parks, French restrictions seemed all the more prickly. *Défense j'inscris ton nom!*

He always felt nostalgic about the days "on the bum," when he had neither possessions nor home. "With that bottle between my legs and the sun splashing through the window I experience once again the splendor of those miserable days when I first arrived in Paris, a bewildered, poverty-stricken individual who haunted the streets like a ghost at a banquet" (*Tropic of Cancer*). No rendezvous, no dinner invitations, no social calendar. He could go off as he pleased, with no plan in mind, and simply sit on a bench in the Tuileries, "getting an erection looking at the dumb statues" (ibid). When he got more experienced at his vagabondage, he even offered advice to the uninitiated.

A Paris street was the greatest teacher of all. Henry was an indefatigable walker, as absorbent as a sponge, and infinitely curious about people and things. Everything he observed was recorded for future use — faces, movements, gestures, odors, passions, sins. What most flattered Henry about the homage Cendrars later paid to *Tropic of Cancer* in "Unto Us An American Writer Is Born" was Cendrars's contention that he'd never read a book by an American, nor by any foreigner for that matter, with descriptions of Paris's streets that could match Henry's. They were incomparable. Among French writers, only Léon-Paul Fargue captured the poetry of the streets in such depth. Passionate about the bistros, cafés, bars, canals, stations, bridges, trains, and dark alleys, Fargue, the *Piéton de Paris* as he was called — the Parisian Pedestrian — had much in common with Miller. He loved "as he would his mistress" the run-down districts, the neighborhoods on the city's outer fringes, and most especially Paris as it looked at night: the windows that lit up or hid misery, the dives packed with drunks and whores, from which shafts of light, familiar melodies, and streams of obscene epithets spilled out into the street.

To remember everything he saw, everything he felt, Henry worked like a man possessed. He sometimes woke before dawn to watch Paris wake — to hear the birds chirping in the squares, the concierge's canaries singing in their cages behind the lace curtains; to see the fruit-and-vegetable seller setting up his still lifes; to watch the butcher spreading out his choice cuts; to smell the freshly baked bread and croissants; to attend the deafening screech of the barber lifting the metal gate to his shop. "There are scarcely any streets in Paris I did not get to know," he wrote in "Remember to Remember." "On every one of them I could erect a tablet commemorating in letters of gold some rich new experience, some deep realization, some moment of illumination."

Paris became to him a "mother, mistress, home, and muse," and Miller tried to fathom what it was about the city that inspired such tender passion. Was it the streets and houses, with their almost human faces? The old stones? The trees, the cafés, the boutiques, the bistros? The more Miller reflected on it, the more he realized that the sources of Parisian magic were innumerable, intangible, and ineffable. *L'Air de Paris*, he thought, was not only in the air, but in the cobblestones and soil, the flesh and blood of the people. You became part of it with the bread you ate, the coffee you drank. It was insubstantial, but it wafted its way down into the smallest details of French life, and once he smelled it, he would never forget: "Walking the streets of Paris the book shops and art galleries never cease to remind one of the heritage of the past and the fever of the present. A random jaunt through one little quarter is sufficient often to create such a glut of emotions that one is paralyzed with conflicting impulses and desires. One needs no artificial stimulation, in Paris, to create. The air is saturated with creation" ("Remember to Remember").

During his "bum" period, Miller turned up in Montparnasse almost every evening, looking for that charitable soul who might take him in. One evening he might stay with Perlès, another with Fraenkel, who was living in the Villa Seurat, a third with the vendor of Indian pearls on Rue Lafayette. Sometimes he slept out under the stars. For many years he had only one permanent address: 11 Rue Scribe, the location of the American Express office. To get there from Montparnasse, you descended Boulevard Raspail, crossed the Seine at Pont-Royal, traversed the Tuileries to the Avenue de l'Opéra, then up to Rue Scribe. By taxi, car, subway, bus, carriage, and most often on foot, every American who has ever lived in Paris, from Gertrude Stein to Fitzgerald, Isadora Duncan to Hemingway and Steinbeck, has trod this path of hope and dreams.

Once, after Henry and I and a beautiful American named Olive had spent a whole night in a nightclub, we realized we were broke, so we made the ritual pilgrimage to this mecca of traveler's checks and dollars. A pile of letters was waiting for Olive in her box. Outside American Express, we hailed a carriage, having no idea how we would pay for it, and during the ride back to Montparnasse, Olive ripped open one letter after another, scanned them quickly, then tore them into tiny pieces, which were flung out the window and carried off by the wind, falling like confetti on the Tuileries lawns. She went through nearly the whole pile and found nothing. Then a miracle occurred. Like a fish breaking the surface of the water, a crisp green bill rose up between Olive's fingers, emerging to our great joy from one of the last envelopes she opened. Ten dollars. No fortune, perhaps, but enough to pay the carriage driver and buy us all a decent breakfast.

How many times did Henry trudge off to the American Express — sometimes several times a day — hoping to find a small check waiting for him, or better still, a money cable or a promissory note. Sometimes he got to 11 Rue Scribe at dawn, then waited impatiently for the tellers to open their windows, which they always did precisely at the stroke of nine. "Each morning the dreary walk to the American Express, and each morning the inevitable answer from the clerk" (*Tropic of Cancer*).

III

Hôtel des Terrasses

At our first meeting, Henry and I exchanged only a few
words. His French was very rough, and I spoke almost no
English. Miller had read a few French books in the United
States — notably Blaise Cendrars's *Moravagine* — but with
painful slowness, needing to look up every other word in a
dictionary. In 1931 he read Céline's *Voyage au bout de la nuit*
[*Journey to the End of Night*] in the same way. Soon, however,
he had a wonderful professor, Monsieur Antelme, from the
South originally, formerly a secretary to Anaïs Nin's father.
Antelme had also given lessons to Anaïs. He was a remarkable man. Henry thought that he embodied the spirit and
character of the French provinces.

Linguistic obstacles did not keep Henry and me from
liking and even understanding each other right away. In love
and friendship, affinities can be silent and do without the
help of words. Henry also thought this was true: "I think that
one day or other," he told Georges Belmont, "writing will
give ground to some other form of expression. I think we'll

all end up by communicating without words." When it was necessary, Fred Perlès acted as an interpreter, and later Frank Dobo, the literary agent, who moved into my hotel. At the time I was trying to finish *Paris by Night*, my first book of photography and a study of Paris lowlife. Miller was insatiably curious about the project, and often came to see me at the Hôtel des Terrasses, which was located on Rue de la Glacière in the 13th arrondissement. For hour after hour he pored over my nightly harvest of photographs, which were stretched out across the bed: the images of dark streets permeated by fog and white mist, the vivid, luminescent reflection of the light from streetlamps on cobblestones, or on the Seine's black water, flowing under the bridges. Between what I gleaned from the night and the Paris he himself loved, Miller found such kinship that one day he handed me an essay titled "The Eye of Paris." Here is what I found written inside:

> And when one day the door was finally thrust open I beheld to my astonishment a thousand replicas of all the scenes, all the streets, all the walls, all the fragments of that Paris wherein I died and was born again . . .
>
> How then am I to describe these morsels or black and white, how refer to them as photographs or specimens of art? Here on this man's bed, drained of all blood and suffering, radiant now with only the life of the sun, I saw my own sacred body exposed, the body that I have written into every stone, every tree, every monument, park, fountain, statue, bridge, and dwelling of Paris. I see now that I am leaving behind me a record of Paris which I have written in blood — but also in peace and good will . . .
>
> Tenderly, reverently, as if I were gathering to my breast the most sentient morsels of myself, I pick up these fragments which lie on the bed.

At the time he wrote this, Miller was sending letters to Dobo with his reactions to my photographs, and the associations and memories they sparked. I had no idea these letters existed until I came across them forty years later. Reading them now is like looking at my reflection in a faraway mirror. There may be those who will think me presumptuous if I quote from these letters, but the person about whom Henry writes has become almost a stranger to me. And besides, how can I hope to capture Miller if I don't report the naked truth about our own relationship?

★   ★   ★

"Since it is impossible for me write in French" — so begins the first letter Miller wrote to Dobo about me, in June 1933 —

> I ask you at the same time to convey my sincere good wishes to cher Halasz.[1] Say that I expect to call on him some afternoon at the hotel and have another look at his marvellous [sic] collection of photos. Meanwhile I am planning to make a niche for him in this present book. As it may be a very wild, a very lavish, a very extravagant portrait I should like to know if he would prefer me to use another name than Brassai in referring to him? I want to include him for two reasons — first, in honest tribute to his talent, second, because one of the principal themes of my book is the "street," and in cher Halasz I find a counterpart to myself, find a man whose curiosity is inexhaustible, a wanderer like myself who seeks no goal except to search perpetually. If you should ever get to read my "Tropic of Cancer" (which Kahane is to print) you would perhaps better understand my sentiments. In that book I conveyed

---

[1] Translator's note: Brassaï's Hungarian name was Gyula Halasz.

an impression of the streets of Paris of which the photographs of Paris seem like the perfect illustration. I should like, if possible, to buy a number of prints from Halasz — perhaps a couple of dozen. At any rate, I was profoundly impressed by the extent and variety of his work, by its dazzling inclusiveness. The walls, the griffonages, the human body, the amazing interiors, all these separate and interrelated elements of the city form in their ensemble a gigantic labyrinthian excavation. I hope that I shall be able to do justice to his work in the pages to come!

It seemed a great pity to me, as I followed his fugitive visions, that no one had singled him out for eulogy, that the tepid name of Paul Morand should dominate his book,[2] that he should be photographing sensational crimes for a newspaper,[3] that he should be acting as collector for Salvator [sic] Dali,[4] etc. etc. etc. Time that some one concentrated on him Halasz, and focussed the attention of the public on *him*. And not less than the photographs did I enjoy his disquisitions on Spengler and Faust, on Dali and the Surrealists, and ship-pumpers and the whore-houses. A fine evening, Dobo, even though slightly marred by the cold logic of a Frenchman.

In conclusion, I wish that you would convey this to Halasz also — that he must inspect the *whole* 13th Arrondissement, particularly these portions:

Place Jeanne d'Arc and the streets spoking off from it. The Rue Harvey, which paralells [sic] the Blvd. de la Gare.

---

[2] He's referring to *Paris by Night*, which appeared with an introduction by Paul Morand in February 1933. — *Au.*

[3] I sometimes did some photographs for *Voilà* and *Détective* magazines [true crime — *trans.*]. — *Au.*

[4] I worked closely with Dali on several articles, notably "The 1900 Style," in *Minotaur* magazine. — *Au.*

The Rue des Rentiers (toward six or seven in the evening).

Place des Peupliers — note the houses with stoops, sign reading "Sage Femme — troisieme class" ["Midwife — third class"].

Rue Demesne — and the streets nearby bearing names of physicians.

Place Paul Verlaine, and neighboring streets, such as Rue des Diamants, Rue de Butte aux Cailles.

Rue Tolbiac — follow it out to the end, into the factory district, over the railroad bridge, into the 12th Arr.

The 13th Arrondissement, in my opinion, is the most interesting of all the quarters of Paris — it is a little universe in itself, and the most putrid, the most squalid, the most diseased, the most hallucinating. See it at dinner hour and again at midnight. See it day after day, in rain and sunshine, in good health and bad, with clear head and with hang-over, with a full belly and with gnawing pains of hunger. Make a book of the 13th Arr. alone?

Yours in health, joy and appreciation —

Henry V. Miller

In another letter to Dobo, dated July of that same year, Miller writes:

I should also like to see more of you and of your confrere, Halasz, who fixes on all and sundry his amiable, microscopic smile, who looks on the grating that surrounds the dead trees of Paris with as much relish and curiosity as he employs in studying his man . . .

My appreciation of Halasz is keen, the more so because I feel that he has inflicted us only with his failures thus far. Halasz, should he follow his intuitive bent, might carry us photographically to new light worlds — I'm sure of it! Because even as we remarked last night, he is a man of ideas, one who is not flabbergasted by the rigmarole and the fanfare of technique . . . One day he will bring his camera out into the open, set the flashlight, and paff boom! he will give them all the works. This is how, happily, I regard cher Monsieur Halasz. I am praying for him all the time.

Cordially,

Henry V. Miller

Several days later, Miller sent Dobo the manuscript of *Black Spring* with these lines: "I offer you this so that you might read it as a sort of testimony to my gratitude, gratitude for the friendship that you and Halasz have shown me with such sincerity." He concludes, "It was a great evening the other night, and I enjoyed it to the utmost. Indeed, my head was in a whirl when I finally tumbled into bed."

IV

The Devourer of Books

Henry could look at my photographs, but I couldn't read his works. When I first knew him he hadn't as yet published anything, and *Tropic of Cancer* was still in gestation. Besides, my grasp of English was not strong. Even with "The Eye of Paris," the essay Henry had written about my work — the manuscript of which he left for me at the desk of my hotel one evening — I had to rely on a friend's verbal translation. The little that I could read was disconcerting. His prose was diffuse, baroque, dreamlike. A bizarre mix of novel, essay, diary, poetry, journal, philosophy, obscenity, esthetic, theology — everything pell-mell in arranged disorder. Later, when we were able to exchange ideas, we often had sharp arguments. Anaïs Nin notes in her *Diary* in October 1933: "Henry brought me several photos by Brassaï and told me about the conversations they had had." Miller also recalled them, as we see in the introduction he wrote to my book *Histoire de Marie* [*The Story of Mary*] (1949): "I ran into Brassaï around midnight one night on the Rue d'Alésia. He had been to witness the cremation of his good friend Tihanyi. It was a gruesome experience and he related it to me in all its harrowing details, but not without humor. He had much to tell me that night. For three hours he held me rooted to the spot, in the middle of the Villa Seurat, discoursing on St. Thomas Aquinas and Goethe's *Faust*, which he had just rediscovered." Thirty years later, in a letter to me, Miller could still recall that talk: "Don't forget the long street dialogue you gave me about Goethe and Thomas Aquinas, on coming home from Tihanyi's cremation about two in the morning. If I could reproduce your talk on that occasion I would consider myself a genuine artist. It was out of this world — but all I have now is the flavor and the ambiance, alas."

During one of our talks I happened to reproach Miller for his long-windedness, his repetitiveness, his wandering digressions, which could sometimes seem a thousand miles away from the subject under treatment. Smiling his quiet mandarin smile, he replied that his chaos was completely deliberate, that what he was looking for was neither logic nor order, but something like the overflow of the Mississippi — impetuously rolling down toward the sea, picking up and sweeping away everything in its path, its muddy waves carrying a million odds and ends: uprooted trees, furniture, cadavers. Writing meant being carried away by the current, and he wanted the reader, too, to be taken, to be swept up and then drowned in the torrential onrush of his prose. As he writes in *Tropic of Cancer*, "I . . . love everything that flows: rivers, sewers, lava, semen, blood, bile, words, sentences." "When I begin to write," he would tell me, "I feel like a breakwater has collapsed. Why would I want to stop the onslaught?" I would reply that I conceived of the role of the artist somewhat differently. Rather than giving in to the torrent, the artist should channel it, endowing the formless with form. Imperturbably, Henry would reply, "I have no absolutely no ambition to become an 'artist,' such as you conceive him. I couldn't give a damn about art! I am but a man and I want to express myself completely and without constraints. Once and for all! I do not believe I am a writer. Nor do I have any ambition to write well or to have a pretty style . . . All I know is that there is a force in me that must express itself. So I stammer, I grope, I look for any and all means possible and imaginable . . . You see, my dear Brassaï, I am very far from being what you might call a 'littérateur,' and especially one of the French variety, enamored of logic, clarity, proportion, strict adherence to form. It may be that my works are not literary. Call them whatever you like! I couldn't care less!"

Henry was most sure he was on the right path whenever someone said of his writing that it lacked finesse. He was proud to learn that the reason Gallimard had refused to publish *Tropic of Cancer* was not because of its obscenity, but because it had judged the work's literary value to be too slight. When Miller read Proust, he was surprised there had been such controversy initially about his writing style: "He's completely classical," he wrote Anaïs Nin in March 1932. Still, he felt kinship: "And so, when I read Proust (I am about finished now) I begin to perceive things, things I already knew, things I refused to bring to the surface. Like him, I could cry out in anguish because my instincts are so sure. But like him, the mind deflects me. I can make the most extravagant allowances."

A key word that kept emerging during my talks with Henry was *regress:*

> I don't want to progress, I want to regress. Yes, regress, become more stupid with every day, as stupid as the plants and animals. To get rid, once and for all, of the effects of five thousand years of history, gods, religions,

books, 'great men' ... If I had the power, I would do away
with schools, museums, I would burn all the libraries. I
would even do away with history, that maker of war. *So you
would do away with all civilization, all culture?* Why not do
exactly that? You cling to your idols: Goethe, Nietzsche,
etc. I have mine too, a whole pantheon of them, but I
would offer them all up to the conflagration, every single
one of them ... What have I gained from the enlargement
of my knowledge, the enrichment of my culture. Nothing. I've lost more. Do you know why I called my first
book *Tropic of Cancer?* It was because to me cancer sym-
bolizes the disease of civilization, the endpoint of the
wrong path, the necessity to change course radically, to
start completely over from scratch ... Yes, from scratch,
no question about it, for better or for worse ... What I
want is to halt evolution, to go backward down the path
we have taken, to back to the world before childhood, to
regress, regress, regress, further and further, until we get
to the place we have only lately left behind, where culture
and civilization do not figure ... It is time that we start to
think, to feel, to see the universe in a way that is uneulti-
vated, primitive — but this is also without doubt the most
difficult thing in the world to do.

In 1959, when Miller read Joseph Delteil's *Saint Francis
of Assisi*, he proclaimed with joy that here was a kindred soul
to his, a "modern saint" whom he could venerate even more
than he did Christ. In Saint Francis, Miller found another
preacher advocating "regression": "He wants us to start all
over again from the beginning," he wrote Lawrence Durrell.
"Back to Paradise, no less. One can never go back? Non-
sense, he cries ... For Francis, he says, it was a matter of
throwing overboard, of rejecting completely 30,000 years of
civilization. What he railed against, in praising holy ignorance, was our bookish culture, our crazy, deadly sciences."

I used to argue that such a return to an innocence beyond science and civilization was impossible. There was always that demon technology, irresistibly drawing everything with it — the whole world and all its inhabitants, whether capitalist or communist. How is humanity to escape its servitude? Only a few isolated individuals, a small handful, can do that! But to get out of the nihilist game by the skin of our teeth so that we can try to live quietly in the margins (as Miller would later try to do in Big Sur, only to become disillusioned) what is that but a refusal to participate in our own times? What I heard from Miller about this regression, this mysterious search for an original state, this absorption deep into the entrails of a world of instinct, this escape from the spiritual and the intellectual, was the great voice of protest itself, undermining our whole culture and civilization. It was the voice to which years later — amplified a thousand, a hundred thousand times — the voices of youth in the streets and cafés of Paris would reply resoundingly.

★　　★　　★

What human being doesn't contradict himself? The very man who was preaching innocence and ignorance and expressing his absolute distrust of literature, was also a *devourer of books*. He downed a dozen of them every week. Durrell used to say that Miller read the way a man who is starving eats. He would read in the cafés, in restaurants, in subways, in bed, and, whenever possible, while sitting on the john. He wolfed down the works of Freud and his disciples Adler, Jung, and Rank; any work by Count Keyserling; Oswald Spengler's *The Decline of the West*; he had read all of Shakespeare's plays — and could recite great parts of them by heart; all of Balzac's *Human Comedy*, only retaining *Séraphita* and *Louis Lambert;* he was reading, with wild enthusiasm, the Salavin series, and Zola, Tolstoy, Gorky, Thomas Mann, Hermann Hesse; and especially all the "biggies": Knut Hamsun, Dostoevsky, and Nietzsche — the last, naturally, was his constant bedside companion. And after he had learned enough of the language, Miller devoured French books: Proust, Valéry, and Gide; Claudel and Giraudoux; Jean Cocteau and Paul Morand; André Breton and the Surrealists. These were followed by newly discovered passions: Elie Faure, Blaise Cendrars, Jean Giono, and of course Céline's *Journey to the End of Night* (which I will discuss later). And then there were the books on Zen, yoga, Chinese thought, Hindu philosophy, astrology, and travel books about the Far East. He could write to Anaïs Nin that he wanted to demolish all the libraries, and then in the same letter scream that he absolutely had to have a copy of *Lady Chatterley's Lover,* the first volume of *The Decline of the West,* Miguel de Unamuno's *The Tragic Meaning of Life,* Jung's book on the unconscious, Elie Faure's book on India, Keyserling's *Symbolic Figures,* Joyce's *Ulysses,* a book on mythology and Greek theater, another on the Astrides, yet another on Orphic myth. He wanted to reread *The Birth of Tragedy.* He was also trying to get his hands on *Shakespeare and His Time, Memoirs of the Foreign Legion* by I can't remember who, and books on the Greek attitude toward homosexuality and the latest psychological views available on the issue.

Thirty years later, Miller admitted that he was horrified to think how much time he had devoted to reading books that hadn't deserved his attention. But that's how life is, he added philosophically. You're either lucky or unlucky in whom you happen to meet. He estimated that he had read somewhere around five thousand books, of which only fifty had given him something he thought was irreplaceable.

Miller and I had other talks of the sort we'd had about

Goethe and Nietzsche, and about other writers. I was stunned to learn that he was less interested in a book's *meaning* than in what the book awoke in him. His manner of reading was profoundly subjective. He would tell me that the "meaning of words [had] lost all importance" to him. Content was unimportant. What was most important was the "musical enchantment" of the words, whether or not they stuck in his imagination. One idea, one phrase, sometimes even one word, could make him feel strangely exalted. Bergson's *Creative Evolution*, he said, had influenced him deeply, but he also confessed that he hadn't actually understood it at all. The word *creative* in the title almost by itself exercised a magical appeal. It became a kind of weapon, a talisman, a shield. Miller had the same kind of odd relationship with the work of Elie Faure, whose *History of Art* he thought was a "symphony of the world"; its author, he said, was the first true musician the French had produced. The book's music enchanted him. Again, it was not the significance or meanings in the work that struck him, but its heady, rich, living language.

The subjective nature of Miller's approach is even more apparent in his reading of Spengler's *The Decline of the West*, an event that he said was one of the pivotal events in his life. Rather than attempting to figure out what made reading it so pivotal, he preferred to abandon himself to the magic of Spengler's writing: "His thought is music to my ears: I recognize all the hidden melodies." *The Decline of the West* was to him a "grand musical poem," a "poem of the world."

Spengler wrote, in his introduction to the work, "And now, finally, I feel urged to name once more those to whom I owe practically everything: Goethe and Nietzsche. Goethe gave me method, Nietzsche the questioning faculty . . ." These sentences, which begin the final chapter of *Plexus*, haunted Miller, so he tells us, for many years. Curiously, it was the second half of the second sentence that haunted him the most: "Nietzsche the questioning faculty." That phrase, said Miller, "sets me to dancing." What about the first part of the sentence, I wondered, the part about borrowing Goethe's methodology? Did Henry wonder what that meant? Not in the slightest. He simply was not curious about the method Spengler was referring to, or how and why Spengler had applied it to history.

For myself, I cannot help but wonder if it is at all possible to understand what Spengler meant without first knowing Goethe. What did Spengler do in *The Decline of the West*, after all, except apply Goethe's vision of a living organism to history, thereby discovering to his surprise that history was neither "evolution" nor linear "continuity," but that it resembled life: birth, growth, maturation, death. The great civilizations — Chinese, Hindu, Egyptian, Greco-Roman, Arab, and so forth — had blossomed, and then faded, at their given moment in time. As it turns out, the whole structure of Spengler's work rests on the ideas Goethe elaborated in the *Metamorphosis of Plants*, the essay on this metamorphosis in *Essay on the General Methodology of Comparisons in Speculations on Morphology*, and in his works on osteology, comparative anatomy, and homology. Of course one can say that *The Decline of the West* is a "grand musical poem," a "poem about the world," and so forth, but what that does not say is that Spengler is providing a new way of comprehending history and the history of art. Spengler was the first historian of the twentieth century to conceive of history not as a mere chronology of facts, but as a vast territory in which thousand-year-old organisms called "cultures" are hatched and die. Interestingly, Elie Faure had similar ideas at the same time in France. Like Spengler, he found organic stages in the evolution of the great styles and established the same kind of parallels Spengler did, such as between Doric, Ionic, and Corinthian art and

Roman, Gothic, and Baroque art. Did Spengler know Elie Faure? Did Elie Faure know Spengler?

★   ★   ★

One can also find Miller's impressionistic way of reading in his essays on writers. What interested him about these writers was where and how they resembled Henry Miller. He brings to them all the emotions and thoughts that they give rise to in him. Miller's Rimbaud and Miller's D. H. Lawrence are incarnations of . . . Miller. Greece is what reverberates in the Greek part of his soul. Henry was aware of this. Writing about someone else, he thought, was a way of revealing oneself. But, interestingly, if Miller writes about himself when he writes about others, his subjective interpretations allow us to get closer to the essence of a work or an author than does an objective approach. A transfusion takes place: Miller lends them his vitality, his blood.

★   ★   ★

One thing that has always intrigued me about Miller's writing is his haphazard use of images and metaphors. The bolder and more stunning they are, the better their chances of hitting their targets, he believes: "[The] moon busting through the greasy sky like a punctured balloon" (*Tropic of Cancer*). At a lycée, at night, in Dijon: "A silence so intense that it sounds like Niagara Falls in my ears" (*Tropic of Cancer*). "All that I had wanted to write these past fall months was now writing itself out. It oozed out like milk from a coconut" (*Plexus*). In "The Eye of Paris," the basis for Miller's clusters of images is me:

> Eye to eye with this man you have the sensation of a razor operating on your own eyeball, a razor which moves with

such delicacy and precision that you are suddenly in a ballroom in which the act of undressing follows upon the wish. His gaze pierces the retina like those marvelous probes which penetrate the labyrinth of the ear in order to sound for dead bone, which tap at the base of the skull like the dull tick of a watch in moments of complete silence.

And here are others, also taken from "The Eye of Paris":

Not the eye of a shark, nor a horse, nor a fly, not any known flexible eye, but the eye of a coccus newborn, a coccus traveling on the wave of an epidemic, always a millimeter in advance of the crest. The eye that gloats and ravages. The eye that precedes doom. The waiting, lurking eye of the ghoul, the torpid, monstrously indifferent eye of the leper, the still, all-inclusive eye of the Buddha which never closes. The *insatiable eye*.

Looking for an instant into the two eyes of this man, I see therein the image of myself. Two enormous eyes I see, two glowing discs which look up at the sun from the bottom of a pool; two round, wondrous orbs that have pushed back the heavy, opaque lids in order to swim up to the surface of the light and drink with unslakeable thirst. Heavy tortoise eyes that have drunk from every stratum; soft, viscous eyes that have burrowed into the mud sinks, tracked the worm and shell; hard, sclerotic gems, bead and nugget, over which the heel of man has passed and left no imprint. Eye that lurks in the primal ooze, lord and master of all it surveys; not waiting on history, not waiting on time.

At the beginning of our friendship, I found Miller's writing style unnerving. Like those Roman candles that explode in a shower of sparks, which, just as they are about to die out, explode in more sparks, and then more again, his images explode and obliterate, overlapping each other with baroque profusion. I had thought that for an image to hit its mark, it needed to be isolated, and set off against a gray or neutral backdrop. Proust also loved to amass metaphors when sometimes only a single image, judiciously chosen, would have sufficed. He multiplied metaphors from a fear that by itself one wouldn't illuminate every facet of a subject, couldn't render the subject in its totality. At first I had the impression that the profusion in Miller's writing, rather than provide greater illumination of its subject, made it seem more distant. It took me some time to understand that the author of the *Tropics* never intended images to illuminate a subject; he used the subject to spawn a whole new generation of images. The image becomes an end in itself, an autonomous creation. Language grows freely, swelling and foaming from ceaseless fulguration. The onward rush plunges words into a frenetic saraband, hurling them far, far away from where they started. Miller's work takes us on a long, hallucinogenic voyage through the tissues and bones and organs of a body, all the way to the backbone. By journey's end, who can remember that it all began with the simple description of one photographer's eyes?

V

Anaïs

It always seemed that just when Miller's life had become precarious, Providence rescued him. In 1931, Providence took the form of a young American lawyer who worked at the Paris branch of the National City Bank: Richard Galen Osborn, "Dick" to his friends, and the "Fillmore" of *Tropic of Cancer.* A born bohemian and blessed with some writing talent, Osborn often spent his evenings in Montparnasse, and it was there that he met Miller. He was immediately fascinated by this man brimming with energy, frothing with wit, and often put Miller up in his apartment at 2 Rue Auguste-Bartholdi, near the Champ-de-Mars, the Ecole Militaire, the Eiffel Tower, and the Quai de Grenelle. A young Russian woman named Irène, who would be a "princesse" named Macha in *Tropic of Cancer,* also spent nights there. Henry normally got up before Osborn and — as soon as he had scraped together enough coins for breakfast and a pack of cigarettes — he set out to explore the new neighborhood. He found the area around the Ecole Militaire

very stiff, and much preferred the small, leprous, and boun-
tiful streets of the 15th arrondissement, farther to the west,
beyond the elevated subway. He especially loved to climb
the length of Rue de Lourmel. His description of it in *Tropic
of Cancer* is perhaps the most beautiful that has ever been
written about a Parisian street.

During bad weather, Henry stayed in Osborn's studio,
and from the window that faced on the cavalry barracks, he
watched the "lunacy" of what went on in the courtyard.
Here is the description of it in *Tropic of Cancer:* "It seemed
incomprehensible to me. Everything done according to
schedule, but a schedule that must have been devised by a
lunatic. There they were, foundering around in the mud, the
bugles blowing, the horses charging — all within four
walls . . . A madhouse, it seemed to me."

A lawyer, Osborn happened to represent the interests of
a young woman from Louveciennes named Mrs. Ian Hugo,
who, to escape her drab surroundings, wrote constantly. She
had just finished an essay on D. H. Lawrence and hoped to
publish it at her own expense. Each time he visited her,
Osborn talked to her about this wonderful, crazy American
he was housing, and who was in the middle of writing a
monumental, thousand-page novel in which every taboo
subject would be featured. When he told her the writer's
name, she exclaimed, "Henry Miller? But I've seen something by him!" She remembered having read an article about
Buñuel's *Golden Age* by someone of that name. Yes, yes, that
was it. She had read it and been struck by the savage,
primitive exuberance of the prose.

Osborn also told Miller about this gifted young woman,
and one day he gave Miller the manuscript of her study of
D. H. Lawrence. Miller, who felt profound admiration for the
author of *Lady Chatterley's Lover,* read it and thought it filled
with earthy truths and original observations, all judiciously

and delicately expressed. The great day arrived — in October 1931 — when Osborn formally introduced them to each other. By this point they were very anxious to meet. Two years later, when he was living in Clichy, Miller began to write his own essay on Lawrence, later publishing it under the title *The Wisdom of the Heart*, and as a way of thanking Osborn for the two great favors he had done for him, Miller dedicated it to him: "To Richard Galen Osborn, originally of Bridgeport, Connecticut, who rescued me from starvation in Paris and set my feet in the right direction. May Heaven protect him and guide him safely to port." (Providence did a poor job. Osborn ended up in a psychiatric ward.)

Daughter of the Spanish pianist and composer Joaquin Nin and the soprano Rosa Culmell, Mrs. Ian Hugo, alias Anaïs Nin, was Parisian by birth, American by nationality, Spanish on her father's side, and Franco-Danish on her mother's. Such a complicated heritage, the product of so many nationalities, languages, customs, thoughts, all of which exerted their influence on her from the cradle, had sharpened her sensibility and refined her intelligence to such a point that she was an *astral* creature — an expression she preferred to *lunatic*. She had spent her childhood drifting from one school and pension to another throughout Europe, and her life had been turned upside down when her father, an unrepentant Don Juan whom she adored, very suddenly left home to sleep his way around the world. Beginning at the age of eleven, hoping that her confessions might reach her absent father and soften his heart, even bring him home to the bosom of his family, Anaïs confided her woes to her *Diary*.

Leaving their villa in Arcachon, her mother took the children to the United States, but in 1920 Anaïs returned to Europe and, having married a businessman in 1929, settled down to live in Louveciennes, in a quiet house once lived in by Turgenev. Left to her own devices, the frail, hypersensitive young woman continued to write in her diary. She clung to it as if it were a life preserver, locking it away in a safe as her most precious treasure. The number of volumes grew and grew. At the point when Henry entered her life, the *Diary* of Anaïs Nin consisted of no fewer than forty-two volumes.

Henry was enchanted from the moment of his first dinner in Louveciennes. He laughed heartily when he admitted to Anaïs that the main reason he had come was in hopes of getting a good meal. After all the sordid miseries of his life on the bum, Henry was delighted to discover the refinements of the French bourgeoisie. Among the sparkling crystal of the glasses, the bookshelves stocked with books, the honeysuckle and nightingales in the lush garden, he found a "splendid feeling of peace and security." And as for Anaïs, she wrote in her *Diary* that "Everything made [Henry] happy: the food, the conversation, the wine, the sound of the clock in the hallway, the way Banquo's tail kept banging into the furniture." She pronounced that this man — so direct, so open, so naked — was a "fabulous animal," the very incarnation of spontaneity. "Nothing he says is premeditated. He never closes off what he thinks or feels." In this young woman, so young, pretty, and intelligent, with such remarkable intuition, cloistered in her house and in her *Diary*, but burning with the desire to escape, drinking in every word he uttered as if he were Pan, Miller found an ideal conversation partner, a mirror to reflect his thoughts, a will prepared to fly to him. Later, Anaïs would admit: "I was not myself with Henry, I was playing the role of the ideal confidante." He thanked her profoundly for her hospitality, and later for her praise: "I am where Proust was, only with more complications, more facts, more mysteries, more terrors, more of everything, except genius.

You almost make me weep with your flattering words. No, I am far from being the artist you imagine. Maybe there are in me possibilities — they have not yet come to fruition. But your friendship, your wonderful sympathy is everything . . ."

Anaïs envied Miller's messy life, in all of its vulgarity and grossness. She wished that she could also destroy the past, spit on the old pieties, escape from her guilt and remorse, and go slumming. She was not cut from the same cloth as Miller, however. Her nature and education held her back. Only Henry would be able to help her to fly with her own wings, so that she could try everything, see everything, feel everything: travel, pleasure, creativity, drunkeness, and even drugs.

The idea that they should exchange came naturally to Henry, who was an inveterate letter writer, and it unleashed a flood of correspondence. Each party to it hurried to explore the universe of the other. Miller's letters were stimulating, exuberant, revealing, and arrived in such rapid succession that they literally submerged her.[1] "I had just sent off a reply," she writes, "and another has arrived." But these missives gave her a "very rare feeling of plenitude," and replying to them gave her enormous pleasure. What enthusiasm about everything! What powerful writing! It was like a torrential stream of fiery lava, obliterating all the hypocrisy, lies, fears, and pettiness that lay in its path. Anaïs was moved by Henry's violence, his fierce appetite for living, his virile sensuality. This spiritual daughter to D. H. Lawrence — now displaced by Miller — who measured people not by their wit or intelligence but by

---

[1] As before, Miller kept his benefactress continually up to date on his projects and ups and downs, and his correspondence with Anaïs Nin would be as important as the one Joyce kept with Harriet Weaver. — *Au.*

their blood and vitality, thought that Miller was her savior. Had he not come, she exclaimed with joy, to discover that part of herself which had remained undeveloped, which needed only to be picked up, educated, guided? "I listen to Henry like a child and he talks to me like a father." In a curious passage in her *Diary*, Anaïs admits to being hypnotized by manly men, by hard "rough types." A shiver of sensual attraction overcomes her, the desire to experience the brutality of men. "To be raped may be a woman's secret erotic need." She adds, "Henry's work has that effect on me" (*Diary*, vol. 2).

Emboldened by their correspondence, Miller sent Anaïs some pages from the novel he'd been working on day and night. Anaïs had appeared in Miller's life at the crucial moment when *Tropic of Cancer* was erupting. He was worried that his "coarse novel" might offend the sensibilities of this sensitive creature. Anaïs was not shocked by what Miller told, but intrigued. She had so little experience in these matters that the most obscene passages were almost meaningless to her. She felt embarrassed and even ashamed at her own innocence. What would Henry think? He might conclude she was being even more forward than earlier. Had she not posed nude for painters at the age of sixteen? "I looked in the dictionary," she confessed, "for some of the words that he used, and couldn't find them." Soon she was writing, "The pages on ecstasy are the most passionate that I have ever read. It is the height of ecstatic literature." Miller sometimes played the role of tutor, and even reprimanded Anaïs. When she denigrated Dostoyevsky and Nietzsche for being "conceited," he asked her to "change something down there." When she remarked that Dos Passos wasn't "human" he replied, "I have just the opposite feeling! I find him warm and friendly!" When she wrote, "the most eternal pages," he replied by saying, "'Eternal' cannot be preceded by *most*. Either something is eternal or it isn't."

★   ★   ★

When Anaïs took the forty-eight notebooks of her *Diary* out of the metal strongboxes and showed them to Miller, he was stunned. He couldn't believe that since the age of eleven she had been spinning a web that, little by little, had imprisoned her. What did she think writing in these notebooks would accomplish? Forge a connection with life? He thought not. All they really did was create a gulf between her and the rest of the world. She wasn't living; she was spending her life contemplating her soul, giving even the smallest incident the proportions of a world-shaking event. How could she live life if she persisted in noting down everything she did and thought? Trying not to seem cruel, Henry nonetheless told Anaïs that these confessions, to which she had devoted heart and soul for so many years, were "bloody ejaculations," and urged her to have done with the *Diary*: He thought she should drive a nail through it and hang it on the wall. When Fred, Henry, and later Durrell referred to the *Diary*, they called it the "monster," or the "whale." In a letter to Anaïs, Miller called it a "Neptunian atlas" and the "ark and covenant of the lost." The well-known psychoanalysts Allendy and Rank, to whom Anaïs had talked about her neuroses, also felt her *Diary* did more damage than good. If Anaïs was cut off from the world, they said, it was because of her morbid and even pathological obsession with writing in the *Diary*. So long as it played the part of her confidant, psychoanalysis could do nothing to cure her.

Deeply shaken though she was by these attacks, Anaïs wouldn't abandon the *Diary*. Nothing more than male vanity, in her opinion, was the cause of all this hostility. Men were nervous about having their little sins and weaknesses noted down day after day by a perceptive woman. (Actually, looking at the *Diary*, the opposite seems true. Her portraits of men are often little more than pure flattery.) And as for the famous psychiatrists, the so-called transference was simply going in the opposite direction, and what the psychoanalysts were revealing were their own neuroses about their own miserable lives. Lawrence Durrell, with whom Anaïs discussed Henry's hostility, also thought that Miller's attitude toward the *Diary* might be driven by personal motives. Perhaps, he suggested, Henry was none too happy that Anaïs was writing down everything he did, every joke and every contradiction. I myself don't believe this. If ever on the face of the earth there lived a man willing to reveal his weaknesses and contradictions, that man was Henry Miller.

All that the disagreements over the *Diary* really did was cause it to swell over the years until eventually it overwhelmed the protagonists. Anaïs sets up two conceptions of autobiography, and they conflict, even though both are based on truths: the first involves a literature of immediacy — spontaneous, born of and in the present; the other a literature of deferment in which, when the facts arrive, they are decanted, filtered, transposed, and elaborated upon through a long process of mental gymnastics involving recollection, memory, imagination, and art.

In Miller's mind, this brought into play a fallacy that made the immediate inscription of actions and facts an illusory act: to commit the events of one day, or even of one hour, to paper takes days if not weeks. Anaïs would therefore never catch up with events, and her *Diary* would never be truly current. Moreover, all she was doing by trying was postponing the exhilaration of life, the moments in whose heat you would never think of writing. The pulse of life makes any formulation impossible. André Gide maintained that when he was living intensely his diary was put out of a job. All the diary can reflect are life's stagnant periods, what André Breton called the "empty moments" of existence. Anaïs wouldn't always avoid throwing herself into the current of life. She too would directly confront the dilemma of whether to live or to write. She herself says as much in her *Diary:* "The river of life divides into two branches: being and formulating" (*Diary,* vol. 2).

Miller concurred with Marcel Proust that immediacy and spontaneity were of less literary value than the subterranean transformations — geological, mineralogical — wrought upon experience by the slow labor of time. Anaïs was in absolute disagreement with this. She wanted to stay on the level of the *untransformed, untransmuted, untransposed.* She held to the truth of the moment. It was the only authentic one. Once it has been forced through the filter of the imagination and memory, reality changes into something entirely different. The context and contents of events and characters, their very nature, are modified. Nothing of the original will survive; all that remains is exaggeration, inflation, and parody. To create in the way that Proust or Henry did, she felt, meant warping and falsifying, distancing oneself from the truth. Everything that creation does, it does to the detriment of the only truth, *the truth of the moment.*

Anaïs began to envision Miller as her antipode: "Henry is becoming unreal. Nothing warm and living remains. The artist. Transmutation. The inhuman transposition of life into memory. He doesn't live in the present. He always has to remember who he is" (*Diary,* vol. 2). What is happening is nothing less than the rejection of art in the name of truth. "This state — artistic creation — that I understand and admire as an artist myself, or in other artists, I do not wish to know it. I want to stay inside *untransformed* human life."

What Anaïs strove for is reflected in the deep hunger of

our own times to capture life at its source, in its immediacy, and without the intermediary of the artist, whether that artist is brilliant or boring. Photography, film, radio, television, are they not specifically intended to do just that? What is current chips away at those venerable, thousand-year-old cliffs of art. Even the most mediocre photographs contain something unique and irreplaceable, something that no Rembrandt, Leonardo, or Picasso — no masterpiece and no artist, living or dead — can attain or equal or replace.

Anaïs went in the opposite direction from Miller and Proust. She searches for the "eternal moments" not in the reminiscence or in the "ruminescence," but in the very same instant and life as the spirit of photography. "I must prove that instantaneous art is possible, art that is immediate, spontaneous, before it goes along the passages of the brain and before lived experience becomes an abstraction, a fiction, a lie." Where Henry wanted to amplify life's events, to exaggerate them via imagination and memory, to push them into the realms of fiction and myth, Anaïs wanted to work only with the unelaborated truth, with what could be caught on the wing.

Curiously, however, if the *Diary* survived despite all this, its character slowly began to change. Miller had released Anaïs from her solitude and plunged her into life, and the result was that the *Diary* became less and less confidential and compensatory, and increasingly a chronicle of facts and events. Sadness and disenchantment disappear, and along with a more objective view of things — a sign of recovery — humor begins to appear.

Twenty years later, in the introduction to the first volume of *The Diary of Anaïs Nin*, published in New York, Miller compared her "monumental confession" to those of Saint Augustine, Petronius, Abelard, Rousseau, and Marcel Proust. No faint praise! One wonders how he could have forgotten how fierce his attempt to destroy the *Diary* had been, and how he had used the poisoned arrows of his sarcasm to shake Anaïs's faith in her undertaking. Had he not advised her to nail the "whale" to the wall to shut it up once and for all?

Although founded on differences, even profound differences, rather than affinities, the friendship between Henry and Anaïs, despite the shadows that briefly crossed its path, would never be denied. It was nothing if not a fertile friendship for them both. Anaïs Nin, this Cinderella who had lived in the margins of her *Diary*, found in Miller a savior who would take her into the heart of life and broaden her horizons. And without Anaïs, would *Tropic of Cancer* ever have appeared?

VI

Exile in Dijon

While Henry faced his unending monetary difficulties philosophically and even enthusiastically, the "Miller problem"
had begun to weigh heavily on the shoulders of his friends.
Prickly as he was about his dignity, Henry began to have the
"painful impression" that this situation could not continue,
that he could not live forever at the expense of his friends.
He had tried to earn a living with his pen, offering his work
to several American magazines, including *Story, Esquire,* and
Liberty, but without success. Finally someone advised him to
go visit a Dr. Horatio Sheafe Krans, director of the International Institute of Education, a kind of Franco-American
friendship organization, and ask him for a job. Just after
Christmas of 1931, the good doctor, while warning Miller
that his administration would soon be "spartanized," offered
him a job as an English tutor in a lycée in Dijon called
Carnot. Miller recoiled at the offer, but, having approached
Krans in the first place, he felt he could not say no, and he
grumblingly accepted the job. He thought that everyone

would be relieved to see him go. One can only imagine his distress at having allowed himself to accept regular work. The horror, the horror! After he had left Western Union, where, between 1920 and 1924, he had been employment manager of the messenger department, he had vowed that never again would he work for anyone.

From the very first, his sojourn in this provincial French city, in the dead of winter, was a disaster. Dijon not only disappointed but frightened him. "Silent, empty gloom — that's how it impressed me," he wrote in that part of *Tropic of Cancer* that deals with the Dijon episode. The cafés were like morgues, the lycée where he taught was depressing, and the other teachers were unfriendly. I still find Henry's unhappiness in this fair capital of the dukes of Burgundy painful — painful that the seat of John the Fearless, Philip the Good, and Charles the Reckless left him feeling indifferent. He probably didn't even know their names, or those of Bossuet, Rude, and Rameau, more favorite sons of Dijon. Dijon is also the gastronomic capital of France and home to all those burgundies that Henry so loved. That alone should have earned it his indulgence, if not his favor. Life sometimes presents such mishaps, when nothing works as it should, and when hostility and misunderstanding get dumbly in the way of our falling in love with those things that, in a happier moment, we otherwise would have. I wish I could picture Henry drinking a Meursault *cassis*, and feeling delighted rather than dismal about his stay in Dijon. He should have gloried in Rabelaisian feasts featuring the "Three Glories" — Dijon, Beaune, and Clos-Vougeot! Ah me. But no, in the winter of 1932, Henry saw Dijon as little more than "a jerkwater town where mustard is turned out in carload lots, in vats and tuns and barrels and pots and cute-looking little jars." In fact, the only thing he could smell was mustard, and it was with a pen dipped in vinegar that he wrote several very funny and poisonous pages about the whole ill-fated experience.

From the very moment he arrived in Dijon, he felt like an exile and an outcast. Taking the job had been a ghastly mistake. All he thought about was returning to Paris, sharing Fred's bed and board (or whoever's), and going back to his old life of cadging. Speaking of which, he had come up with several ingenious new ideas — including composing a list of the names of people who might invite him to dinner, one right after the other, one for every day of the week.

Happily, he only had two or three hours of class each day, and these consisted entirely of conversation. In his free time, with the help of a dictionary, he read Proust's *Albertine Disappeared*. The Café Miroir proved an excellent place to read — comfortable and well heated and without the female orchestra that set his teeth on edge. "On a winter's night, in a dirty hole like Dijon, nothing can be more harassing, more nerve-racking, than the sound of a French orchestra. Particularly one of those lugubrious female orchestras with everything coming in squeaks and farts, with a dry, algebraic rhythm and the hygienic consistency of toothpaste." Miller was never lucky enough to meet one of those Madame Bovarys that he was convinced had to be around someplace in the Côte-d'Or region. Instead, he amused himself by infecting the school staff with the "Spengler Virus" and by winning the devotion of his students with a course he gave on Remy de Gourmont's *Physique de l'amour*, of which certain passages involving a bear's penis would figure in *Tropic of Cancer.*

Only the daily banter of his colleagues at dinner offered any real pleasure, primarily because it was as scatological and lascivious as his own. He had the marvelous opportunity to learn from these exchanges of smut and filth the entire repertory of the French gutter. Miller felt as if he had been dropped into Rabelais's medieval world of students, and he mined the vulgar and licentious discourse of the teachers' lounge for everything it was worth. He met a young man of twenty-one named Jean Renaud, who went on to become a teacher. "Wrapped in his cowl like a gluttonous monk," Renaud talked to him about German philosophy and the work of Goethe, the centenary of whose death they were celebrating in 1932. Even if he knew something about German literature, Renaud couldn't speak a word of English to save his life, so Henry had to stumble along in French. Passionate about architecture, Renaud initiated him into the Roman and Gothic architecture Dijon has in such abundance, and notably Saint-Michel, whose armies of gargoyles, plastered on its façade, qualify it as one of France's oddest churches. Henry thought Renaud's discourses on Dijon as marvelous as Marcel Proust's on Normandy's churches. This young teacher also saw to it that Miller taste — the event of a lifetime — one of the most prestigious of the burgundies: a bottle of Latricière-Chambertin, with which the dukes of Burgundy in their caves swore their allegiance.

After three weeks, Henry was suddenly delivered. Fred sent a telegram announcing that the *Chicago Herald Tribune* was looking for a proofreader and that the job was his. Henry wondered with considerable anxiety if this new job wouldn't be worse than the one in Dijon, if he wasn't simply leaving one purgatory for another.[1] At least he'd be in Paris rather than in this depressing backwater. In the end, without so much as a word of warning to either his colleagues or his students, Miller left the school and the capital of Burgundy and fled back to Paris.

---

[1] Translator's note: In *Tropic of Cancer,* Miller reverses the proofreading job and the position at the Lycée Carnot in Dijon, which comes at the very end of the novel. After he has accepted the teaching job, he wonders (p. 263) if it wasn't "just a transfer from one purgatory to another."

VII

The Night Job

I'm imagining Henry sitting in a tiny cubicle in an office building in the heart of Paris. Around him is the clickity-click of linotypes, the clackety-clack of the arms moving across the spin-dryer, the roar of printing-press motors, the heat from hot lead, the smell of paper and printer's ink. Miller the schoolteacher has become Miller the newspaperman, busily adding punctuation to press reports and cables from New York, Tokyo, Moscow, and London, all filled with news of earthquakes, explosions, riots, fires, accidents, cyclones, floods, famines, assassinations, shipwrecks, wars, and revolutions. Feeling as if he were made of stone, unfeeling, he works away at them. Nothing can reach him, nothing moves him. "I am inoculated against every disease," he writes in *Tropic of Cancer,* "every calamity, every sorrow and misery."

While he was waiting — and as was his custom — he turned his little cubicle into an observation post. After three weeks in a provincial lycée, he enjoyed observing his Parisian coworkers, listening in on their conversations, spying on them in the bathrooms and decrepit locker rooms where they scrawled their obscene graffiti. Their extreme poverty and lack of hygiene took him by surprise. "Ugh! but they stank, those devils! And they were well paid for it, too. But there they were, stripped down, some in long underwear, some with beards, most of them pale, skinny rats with lead in their veins."

The offices of the *Chicago Herald Tribune*, at 5 Rue Lamartine, were located in the middle of Paris's red-light district. All Henry had to do was walk through the door of Chez Paul, two doors down, and he found himself in the dark heart of the district and among the men who ruled it. How miserable the workers at the press seemed next to these *mecs* — pimps — thought Henry. They sat around twiddling their thumbs like nabobs, lazing their way through the day playing *belote* or shooting dice, while their *poules*, their female partners, walked the streets soliciting business. Henry always spoke of the *mecs* with admiration, even envy, and his portrait of them in *Tropic of Cancer* shows real empathy. Their power over women, their ability to live without either scruples or shame, their sales pitches, their horror at the thought of regular work, all these made them seem brotherly.[1] And it was with pride that he wrote, in his portrait of a Parisian prostitute entitled "Mademoiselle Claude," "I'm the first *maquereau* [*sic*] Claude has ever had. And I don't call myself a *maquereau* either. Pimp's the word. I'm her pimp now. O.K."

Once Miller became a regular at Chez Paul's (he even managed to establish some credit there), he began observing the men in earnest. One *mec*, a "big, blond brute," would eat dinner with one of his girls before she hit the streets. An-

---

1 The hero of his play *Just Wild About Harry* (the title of a song) is a pimp, a good pimp. — *Au.*

other never stopped arguing, and then making up, with his *poule*, the magnificent and gorgeous Lucienne, before she took wing for the sidewalks. What does a *macquereau* think about when his *poule* is out turning tricks? Why, about the money she'll bring back, of course! Didn't the guys she was screwing make him jealous? Henry found himself identifying with these men, obviously remembering the aching jealousy he had felt during those seven years when June would disappear for hours at a time and he didn't know, or want to know, where she'd gone.

Miller's new line of work threw him into the heart of Paris nightlife and lowlife. He went from being an early bird to becoming a night owl. When he walked back to Montparnasse with Fred at two in the morning, they often went by Les Halles, the Tuileries, the Luxembourg Gardens. But, just as often, he walked by himself through Paris's gamier sections, those places where the hunter becomes the hunted. The neighborhoods around Montmartre, and from Rue Lafayette down to the *grands boulevards*, were particularly infested. Walking here, he wrote, was "like running the gauntlet." The prostitutes "attach themselves to you like barnacles, they eat into you like ants, they coax, wheedle, cajole, implore, beseech, they try it out in German, English, Spanish, they show you their torn hearts and their busted shoes . . ." (*Tropic of Cancer*). The truth was that Henry loved being accosted by these batallions of *poules*. He was fascinated with the little bars that were "alive, throbbing, the dice loaded," and where the cashiers "perched like vultures on their high stools." Sometimes he went along Boulevard de la Madeleine, the realm of the higher-priced *poules de luxe*. They reminded Henry of the *bayadères*, Matisse's spectral odalisks. Sometimes he walked all the way down the *grands boulevards* to the Bastille area. Near Rue de Lappe, between Boulevard Beaumarchais and

Rue Amelot, he uncovered a little street of *poules* who, curiously enough, were connected to a preacher named Wagner. Why not? thought Henry. Perhaps Reverend Wagner was delighted to have some Mary Magdalenes working *his* street. Miller often came here to observe the "vultures" perched on their stools in a small bar. At the Café de L'Eléphant he met Germaine, a "whore all the way through" — pure-blooded and aggressive, a true survivor. Unlike the more hesitant Mademoiselle Claude, Germaine had no compunctions about going after and latching on to the *michés*, her johns. Sometimes Henry made a foray into the "belly of Paris" so dear to Zola, drawn by the vegetal animation of Les Halles, the cheeses, flowers, fresh produce, and fruits, but most especially by the colorful army of prostitutes. Gathered together under the porticoes of hotels and around the counters of the small bars, these *filles de joie* in their miniskirts and garish-colored thigh boots launched a style that, years later, would be considered *haute couture* by young women around the world.

It was usually daylight by the time Henry reached Montparnasse. The busy nightspots were deserted. One of the most beautifully grotesque passages of *Tropic of Cancer* describes the day that is rising on Montparnasse:

> In the blue of an electric dawn the peanut shells look wan and crumpled; along the beach at Montparnasse the water lilies bend and break. When the tide is on the ebb and only a few syphilitic mermaids are left stranded in the muck, the Dôme looks like a shooting gallery that's been struck by a cyclone. Everything is slowly dribbling back to the sewer... What hopes there were are swept up. The moment has come to void the last bagful of urine. The day is sneaking in like a leper...

VIII

Clichy Days

One day, Fred announced that he and Henry had decided to live in Clichy. What a ridiculous idea, I thought, to go and live with the devil in one of the seediest suburbs of Paris! After two years of furnished rooms and endless vagabondage, however, Miller wanted very badly to have a home and a permanent address. A real home life had always been irresistibly attractive to this would-be bohemian, but for one reason or another it had always eluded him. He recalls in *Tropic of Capricorn* how he had hated his mother, whom he describes as a "complete stranger"; he might have made a home with his sister if she hadn't been a half-wit, a "harmless monster," or with his father, whom he loved, if he hadn't been a drunk. When he pursued a woman with the idea of setting up house, it usually ended in failure: first, the widow — she could have been his mother — then the pianist, "Maude," the mother of his first daughter, Barbara; and then finally, June, and seven years of "a dance of death," as he calls it in *Tropic of Cancer,* a life characterized by

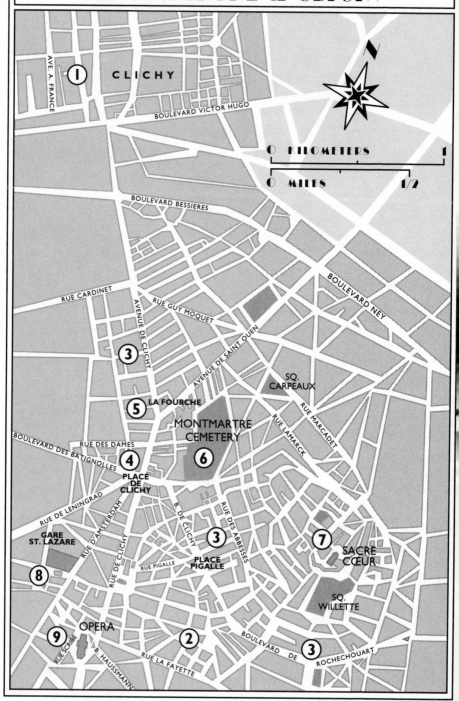

1 "At the end of March 1932, Henry and Fred moved into a small, modest-looking apartment at 4 Avenue Anatole-France. The apartment consisted of two rooms, a kitchen, and a bathroom, and was located a half hour's walk from Porte de Clichy, the last stop on the Métro."

2 "The offices of the *Chicago Herald Tribune,* at 5 Rue Lamartine, were located in the middle of Paris's red-light district. All Henry had to do was walk through the door of Chez Paul, two doors down, and he found himself in the dark heart of the district and among the men who ruled it."

3 "He soon knew all of Avenue Clichy like the back of his hand, as well as the streets and alleys that emptied into it, and also Boulevard Rochechouart. He explored it all, from bottom to top—from the Moulin Rouge to Place Pigalle. The long sequence of cafés, restaurants, cabarets, movie theaters, residence hotels, and twenty-four-hour pharmacies reminded him of that stretch of Broadway between Forty-second and Fifty-third streets. The difference was that Montmartre was even more of a flesh market. With its little dives jammed with prostitutes, pimps, thugs, crooks, and other local color, this boulevard at the foot of Sacré Cœur seemed to him the raunchiest corner in all Paris. Vice lurked over everything like an erotic gargoyle."

4 "On Place de Clichy he found his oasis—the Café Wepler. From the moment he first went there, Henry thought Wepler was nothing less than the epicenter of sex. It reminded him of Broadway's dance halls, in which, when one entered them, one penetrated 'the vaginal vestibule of love.' For two years he made it his home, his principal observation point."

5 "Henry also explored the intersection between Place de Clichy and Porte de Clichy called 'La Fourche.' La Fourche! A prophetic name if ever there was one! Destiny itself must have placed it in the path of the author of the *Tropics*, and it must have been for his benefit alone that Avenue Clichy branched off from Avenue Saint-Ouen, like two widening thighs."

6/7 "'The Cemetery Montmartre. . . shot from the bridge at night is a phantasmagoric creation of death flowering in electricity; the intense patches of night lie upon the tombs and crosses in a crazy patchwork of steel girders which fade with the sunlight into bright green lawns and flower beds and graveled walks' ('The Eye of Paris'). Henry also loved watching the ghostly evaporation of night, giving way to the first glow of day spreading across the city. Sometimes, to better capture this fleeting moment, he prowled through the night all the way up to Sacré Cœur to catch dawn's arrival on a Paris still shrouded in sleep."

8 "Sometimes Henry went as far down as the Saint-Lazare train station to watch prostitutes accost the men, and to see the 'thick tide of semen flooding the gutters'(*Tropic of Cancer*)."

9 "For many years he had only one permanent address: 11 Rue Scribe, the location of the American Express office."

everything save the intimate family life for which he longed. One can imagine how he felt that day when he looked through a window and saw the home of his dreams: a cheerful dining room, a young girl with her nose in a book, the table set for dinner. And every other house on this quiet little street was just like it — the same scene, the same intimacy: a loaf of bread, a bottle of wine, some cheese, a bowl of fruit in the middle of a table around which the whole family sits in a circle, talking away. Henry had never let go of this vision.

He was also in a hurry to find the right place to give birth to the half-dozen books with which he was pregnant. Every event and character from his life, past and present, was pressing in upon him; he needed to open the gates and let them out. Finally, there were financial reasons for choosing a backwater in the middle of Paris's "rust belt." The rents in these neighborhoods were far below what they were in the city proper. For the price of a single room in a Paris fleabag hotel, he and Fred could have an entire apartment in the suburbs.

The questions remains: Why Clichy, the antipode of Montparnasse? Why not more upbeat suburbs such as Montrouse, Arcueil, or Clamart? Céline's *Journey to the End of Night* may have exerted an influence. Louis-Ferdinand's bombshell of a book didn't drop until November 1932, but thanks to Dobo's agenting skills, Henry had had a chance to read the novel in manuscript in 1931, several months before the decision to move to Clichy had been made. The book electrified him. Inspired by Céline, and perhaps also driven by childhood memories, Miller was anxious to move into that grim landscape of smokestacks, gasometers, and slag heaps, to fill his lungs with the suffocating smoke of oil refineries and burning refuse, to walk on broken pavement, and to share his life with the working crowd — in other words, to discover what Pierre Mac Orlan used to like to call the *fantastique social* of the Parisian suburbs. Henry hoped he might get to know Céline, who had lived at 36 Rue d'Alsace for four years while working on his novel. But by the time Henry and Fred set up house there, Céline had already moved to Montmartre. Only his alter ego, Dr. Destouches, still came back every day to care for the patients at the clinic on the Rue Fanny. Twice, I myself went to that clinic, a modern structure located next to the Batignolles cemetery, to photograph Céline and — alas! — missed him both times.

At the end of March 1932, Henry and Fred moved into a small, modest-looking apartment at 4 Avenue Anatole-France. The apartment consisted of two rooms, a kitchen, and a bathroom, and was located a half hour's walk from the Porte de Clichy, the last stop on the Métro. Slightly nervous at the idea of walking around this dangerous area after dark, Fred bought a serrated knife like the ones that the neighborhood thugs used. Henry carried his heavy Mexican cane.

When I met Henry after the move to Clichy (he still came to Montparnasse from time to time), he looked radiant. At long last he had a place of his own. Avenue Anatole-France was Park Avenue, and his monastic little room painted white, consisting of a bed, a table, and a wooden chair, was the most beautiful room in the world. Little by little, the kitchen acquired a full array of frying pans and cooking pots, and even boasted a high-quality cauldron for *pot-au-feu*, Miller's favorite dish. Anaïs, whose visits had become more and more frequent, followed the move to Clichy with curiosity and anxiety. She made a few interior-decorating recommendations, such as moving the couch so that whoever sat there didn't get the sun in his or her eyes, and covering bare lightbulbs with lampshades. Each time she came for a visit, she brought presents for her Henry and Fred, and thanks to her good taste and instinct for comfort and well-being, the Clichy apartment not only looked less and less austere and more and more habitable, but even took on a certain cachet.

Henry's appearance was also changed. He purchased a sturdy pair of work shoes, and was delighted when the salesman he bought them from took him for a worker rather than an American tourist. When Anaïs noticed that Henry still didn't have a winter coat, she had one made for him out of corduroy.

In *Tropic of Cancer*, when Miller lists all the calamities that pass under the nose of a proofreader at the *Chicago Herald Tribune*, he notes that "the greatest calamity for a proofreader is the threat of losing his job." That calamity was visited upon him. When they discovered that he didn't have a visa to work in France, the management let him go, without a single word of warning. "Nothing to do but to get down into the street again, walk, hang around, sit on benches, kill time." Deep down, he was jubilant about having his freedom back.

In the meantime, the good doctor Horatio Sheafe Krans remained concerned about Miller's fate. Krans was apparently not angry about Miller's scandalous desertion of his post at the Lycée Carnot, and even offered Henry several other jobs.

One day in July he sent Henry a note urging him to get in immediate touch with Paul Morand. Paul Morand! Henry was stunned. He looked at the name with tremulous excitement. At the time this great friend of Giraudoux and Marcel Proust was at the height of his literary glory. Céline considered him one of the great prose writers of France — if not the greatest. The author of *Closed All Night* and *Paris de Nuit* was preparing to go on a lecture tour across the United States, and was looking for a young American writer to translate his texts. Even though the offer was not what one would call enticing (five hundred francs to do twenty-five pages) Henry wanted to take it. He had his reasons. He hoped, he told Anaïs, that Morand would introduce him to a publisher. He also worried that his halting French would prevent him from doing a good job with the translation. Fred offered to help him out — if they split the proceeds fifty-fifty. In the end, unfortunately, things didn't work out, but again Henry was not unhappy about it. Unemployment suited him. Besides, Fred and Anaïs were always there to fix him up if something happened. Worrying about money during these days was one's daily bread. Everyone was hitting everyone else up for small amounts. Miller wrote me in 1933: "Dear Halasz, . . . now I need 30 francs. Really and truly. Bring it with you tonight, please, to . . . chez Henry Miller."

At the end of December, that same year, he wrote in his distinctly flavorful French:

> Dear Halasz,
>
> A week ago I come to your place with Fred, because I had a check of Anaïs's containing the 100 francs for you and something for me. Your not being there, I wasted the money of yours!
>
> Today I have another check for 270 francs. It's dated Monday, December 24. I need money urgently and before then. I would like to give you the hundred francs that I owe you. But can you *break* the check at the patron's for example? — Come see me this afternoon, if possible. [Literal translation.]
>
> Henry Miller

Few of my friends at the time had checking accounts, and since I couldn't do anything with the checks myself, I was forced to give them to the manager (the *patron*) of my hotel, who cashed them. This operation had one major draw-back. Before giving me the money, the manager would take out all the back rent I owed him. Sometimes nothing was left over. At any rate, my correspondence with Henry at the time constantly revolved around money problems. Even as late as 1937, Miller — by then the author of three or four published works — was still sending out letters of distress. I've lost some of the most poignant ones, but there are still a few survivors:

> Dear Halasz,
>
> Today completely broke! If you have anything — a ten-franc coin for example, send it to me this afternoon. And I will thank you humbly and joyously and loyally.
>
> Your Miller
>
> (who has not yet died of hunger)

One day in June 1932, Henry and Fred invited me to lunch. When I got to Clichy, Miller was in the process of scrubbing the red tiles of the kitchen with bleach. The same man who had castigated D. H. Lawrence for his servility in matters pertaining to domestic chores — woman's work! — was now cheerfully performing those same chores with what one might have said was a certain abandon. What a sight it was to see him squeezing the last drops out of the washcloth, then dunking it over and over in bleach. "Just like a Dutch washerwoman, right?" Fred said with a sneer. It was just what I was thinking. As soon as lunch was over, Henry cleared the table and started in on the dishes. Plates, pots, dirty glasses piled in the sink. Perhaps it was his German ancestry. In the Miller household in Brooklyn, one always hurried to have done with the dishes so that they could be put back in the cupboard as soon as possible; and after the washing, one ironed the linens and stacked them neatly in the storage chest. Curiously, what had disgusted Henry most about World War I was not so much the suffering and murderous absurdity, but the total absence of sanitary facilities, the disorder, the vermin.

The grilled steak, sprinkled with parsley and marinated in a bottle of Médoc, was excellent. The furnishings gave a feeling of prosperity and security. After lunch, Fred and Henry proudly showed off their new acquisitions: two bright and shiny bicycles, polished, oiled, and ready to set them free. They would go on long bike rides to Saint-Germain, to Louveciennes, sometimes all the way to Versailles or Saint-Cloud. Later they even toured the châteaux of the Loire Valley on bikes and, I believe, also went as far as Luxembourg.

But Henry loved most of all to walk, and it was on foot that he explored the neighboring communities: Saint-Denis, Courbevoie, Aubervilliers, Les Batignolles, and most of all Montmartre. He soon knew all of Avenue Clichy like the back of his hand, as well as the streets and alleys that emptied into it, and also Boulevard Rochechouart. He explored it all, from bottom to top — from the Moulin Rouge to the Place Pigalle. The long sequence of cafés, restaurants, cabarets, movie theaters, residence hotels, and twenty-four-hour pharmacies, reminded him of that stretch of Broadway between Forty-second and Fifty-third streets. The difference was that Montmartre was even more of a flesh market. With its little dives jammed with prostitutes, pimps, thugs, crooks, and other local color, this boulevard at the foot of Sacré Coeur seemed to him the raunchiest corner in all Paris. Vice lurked over everything like an erotic gargoyle. Miller was sorry to see that neon lights were slowly making inroads. His opinion, rendered in his memoir of those times, *Quiet*

Days in Clichy, was that the "sexual life flourishes better in a dim, murky light."

On the Place de Clichy he found his oasis — the Café Wepler. From the moment he first went there, Henry thought Wepler was nothing less than the epicenter of sex. It reminded him of Broadway's dance halls, in which, when one entered them, one penetrated "the vaginal vestibule of love." For two years he made it his home, his principal observation point. In the summer he sat out on the terrace, and in winter, when his fingers were too cold to work the keyboard of his typewriter back in his glacial room, he sat inside the café. Most of the prostitutes who made their way into his works were Wepler habitués.

Some find it surprising that a man whom women found so attractive, and who could conquer with ease, was himself so strongly attracted to prostitutes. But being the bard of physical love, how could he abandon these priestesses to a life of contempt in the gutter? His first real Parisian work appeared in Samuel Putnam's *New Review,* and its heroine was the aforementioned Mademoiselle Claude.

This was another world in which Miller could trace Céline's footsteps. In one of the most beautiful chapters of *Journey to the End of Night,* the latter pays tender homage to the good-hearted Molly, a prostitute from Detroit. Miller thought her portrait one of the most beautiful ever done of a woman. "For the first time a human being was interested in me," says Bardamu in the novel, "in my inner self, if I dare say that, in my egoism. She put herself in my place and didn't judge me the way all the others did." Céline adds, "One is ashamed not to be richer in heart and in everything and still to have judged humanity to be baser than it really is at bottom" (*Journey to the End of Night,* p. 207). Henry felt the same way about Mademoiselle Claude. Delicacy of sentiment and generosity of spirit mean nothing to a prostitute; if anything, they were signs of failure. Yet, through Claude, Miller began to see that these so-called fallen women were something far different from "vultures" and "birds of prey." How many desperate souls had these sisters of mercy not saved? Those who held them in contempt knew nothing of the drama that had forced them out on the streets. Henry admired their courage, their daily acts of heroism without which they could not survive. He loved the open, honest, and direct way they earned a living, as opposed to the "sugary and exhausting tactics of women in high society": "I like prostitutes! They don't put on airs. They bathe in front of you."

Part of the reason for Miller's feelings was that it was prostitutes who taught him French and taught him about France. Each one, he felt, embodied the charm of the region of the country from which they'd come: Mademoiselle Claude was from the Loire; Mademoiselle Nys de Gavarnie from the Pyrenees; Germaine represented Brittany; Lucienne, Normandy. "If the memory of certain *femmes de joie*, as they are justly called, is precious to me," wrote Miller twenty years later in "Remember to Remember," "it is because at their breasts I drank again those strong draughts of mother's milk in which language, landscape and myth are blended." And he adds, "To me they were the little queens of France, the unrecognized daughters of the Republic, spreading light and joy in return for abuse and mortification. What would France be without these self-appointed ambassadors of goodwill?"

Miller also began the habit of doing all his correspondence at cafés. Paper, ink, pen — these were included in the price of a *café crème*. That, he thought, was one of the marvels of Paris. He consumed an enormous quantity of the

"AU PETIT POUCET"
1, Rue Biot - 5, Place Clichy
PARIS (XVIIᵉ)

Consommations de Premier Choix
BUFFET FROID
TABAC DE LUXE

Ouvert jusqu'à 2 heures du matin

TÉLÉPHONE | Numéro d'appel
3 Lignes | Marcadet 12-28

R. C. Seine 322.489

PARIS, le mardi 19 août 1933

Cher Halasz —

Votre livre — est-ce paru? Je voudrais bien acheter une copie — peut-être je peux vendre quelques-uns aussi. Dites-moi qu'est-ce qu'il y a.

Sincèrement,

Henry V. Miller

4, Ave. Anatole France
Clichy (Seine)

P.S. Je viens de compiler mes notes pour les relier dans 2 volumes — notes de mon pèlerinage à Paris cettes trois années passées. Si vous avez une photographie (pas trop grande) serviceable pour un tel livre personnel (quel français!), envoyez le à moi, s'il vous plaît. Je veux payer, comprenez? mais, quelque chose bizarré et silencieux.

Hm.

mes grands amitiés toujours

76

beverage. Nearly all his letters from this period, and there are hundreds upon hundreds of them, carry the letterheads of the cafés around the Place Clichy. One that he addressed to me, and that I believe dates from January 1933, carries the logo of the *café-tabac* called Au Petit Poucet [Tom Thumb], located on the corner of Rue Biot and the Avenue de Clichy:

> I just compiled my notes to bind them in two volumes, notes of my pilgrimage to Paris and these three years spent. If you have a photograph (not too big) usable for such a personal book, send it to me, please. I want to pay it. You understand? But something mottled and silent. [Literal translation. Original reproduced on facing page.]

In the notebooks he refers to, Miller wrote down his dreams, his desires, his dirtiest thoughts, the books he wanted to read, the names of streets, and so forth. I probably didn't answer his letter — as is my habit — so Henry took up the matter again, on March 8, 1933:

> As to the photograph the subject of which I wrote in my last letter, it isn't of great importance. I had wanted an example of your art for a notebook of my memories in Paris. I put in a page of my notebook on which I would blue the photograph. Naturally for a dirty rotten American as I am, I had envisioned a photograph notably sexual. Believe me, dear Halasz, that I am always appreciative of your kindness, good wishes, etc. [Literal translation.]

To this he added a postscript:

> Here at the Café Wepler, one always plays the Lustige Witwe — The Merry Widow — like a monomania of the obsessed. And the singer always sings the same aria from

the *Barber of Seville*: Picoropicoropicoropicoropicoro-picoro!

And a second postscript:

> It's very pretty to be the toilet lady here with all this sweet
> Viennese music. One can imagine oneself in Vienna, or in
> Buxtehude or at the Gare de Lyon.

Most of Miller's letters from this period are written in the same vein as the *Tropic of Cancer*; they sparkle with humor and cascade with images. I'm sorry that so many have been lost — it never occurred to Henry to keep copies — but I'm delighted to reproduce one unpublished letter to Frank Dobo, dated July 27, 1932. Part freewheeling ramble and midnight confession, it provides a sort of balance sheet of his hopes, dreams, and desires. Like Frédéric Moreau in Flaubert's *Sentimental Education*, the young student who dreams of "the love of princesses in satin boudoirs or garish orgies with illustrious courtesans," Miller dreams of "aging actresses," of the "President's mistress," or the "cast-off wife of a celebrated painter." The letter also reveals some of his disappointments about Paris:

> My dear Dobo,
>
> Just before you appeared on the terrasse of the Dome last night I was saying to myself that this coming year I would make it my business to "crash" the portals of society, just to have a glimpse of that life which the French deny us foreigners by erecting their Chinese wall of cafés. I am going to make it my business to cultivate the friendship, or the acquaintance, at least, of a few men of letters, or artists, or society hounds. I am going to do it cold-bloodedly. I want to meet these people on their own

grounds, I want to be wined and dined in an old-fashioned mansion, I want to be driven through the Bois in a sporting car by some racy young society dame who pretends to interest herself in the arts, etc. I want to have an affair with an old actress, or the mistress of the President, or the cast-off wife of a celebrated painter.

Going home last night, a long walk which permitted me to chew over your words about Budapest, I suddenly recalled a story related to me by an American business man who was visiting Budapest. He told me of meeting a young widow of good family along the Danube one evening, of taking her in a taxi to the Island of St. Marguerite, of proceeding then to her home and by easy stages to the bed, and thence remaining domiciled with her for a week, enjoying the bounteous hospitality of the Hungarian people. All this without knowledge of the language, or even an intermediary tongue. How remote, such a situation, from the adventures[?] offered us in Paris! And yet there are infinite possibilities here, if only one is thrown into the right set, the so-called "smart set."

All this sounds banal, and it is. But here it is — after one has been four years in a strange country, without the slightest contact, intimate contact, with her people one begins to get itchy, spiritually, so to speak. I feel as if all the whores I had lain with and all the pimps[?] I have talked with are crawling over me in a St. Vitus dance. I know the French only because I am lousy. I want to be fumigated and given a clean pair of underwear.

Wherefore, in mulling over divers things that occurred last night, and of no moment, the whispered conversation which you had with your office assistant leaped to my mind with strange force. I could not help but overhear your energetic and insistent refusal. You explained to me later the reason for it. I said nothing. But inwardly I smiled somewhat ruefully to myself, a little exasperatedly too. What would I not have given to

exchange places with you! I have known a French telephone operator, or a dactylo, or a salesgirl in a department
store, or a midinette, or a grisette, or a lorette, or a cocotte.
If one of them came my way I would guard her like a rare
beetle, take her home, put her under a glass bell, study
her, pull her wings off, soak her in alcohol or vinegar,
dissect her abdomen and study the geometry of her giz-
zards. . . . . I assure you, my dear Dobo, who appear to be
so unfortunately interested in American customs, that
these things do not occur in our country. A man does not
say no to a woman there, because figuratively speaking we
are all running around with our tongues hanging out.
There is a paucity of women, of lecherous women especially. When one finally carries one off he discovers soon
enough that he has brought home a viper or a tigress. Or
else a Holy Madonna who covers her face with her hands
every time she is violated.

Just before you arrived last night I was really enjoying myself for a moment watching the beautiful new crop
of American tourists swinging by. Not in all the time I
have been in Paris have I seen such a number of superb
females pass in review. They were goddesses. And they
were clothed like goddesses. But one has only to hear
them speak and one is immediately disillusioned. (That is
why I am delighted with the "dubbing" of American
pictures: One has the privilege of looking at animal perfection and listening to a charming tongue. See an "original version" and one comes away puking. When one can
see a beautiful tigress such as Joan Crawford dubbed by a
Damia, for instance, one is accorded a rare privilege. It is
the realization of the legendary hybrid fixation which so
fascinated the Greeks. The day is coming when we shall
see the actualization on the screen of the great centaurs
that dominated the imagination of the Mediterranean
people, from Crete to Egypt.)

As for the girl in green, who sat beside you, permit

me to say candidly that I took her for a whore, and if she is not one she ought to be one — she has missed her calling. No, I did not like her, and I do not like her now, in retrospect. There are some whom time garnishes. She is not one. I detest her indigo dye, her underslung lip, her shapeless avoirdupois, her basilisk stare, her measured words, her not impeccable aloofness, her heavy trot, the sweat under her arms, the smile that she applies like a fixative, the collar of fat around her gills, the ball and chain around her ankles. I detest her from head to foot — because I think she is half-man — and if you protest that she has been violated a thousand times I shall not change my conviction.

But enough of this. Whom would I like to meet this winter? I will tell you. Duhamel, Cocteau, André Gide, Paul Morand, Henri Duvernois, Blaise Cendrars, Marc Chagall, Dufresne, Picasso, Matisse, Raoul Dufy, Colette, Damia, Elvire Popescu, Noel-Noel, Kiki, Rin-tin-tin, Dostoievski, Elie Faure, Oswald Spengler, Thomas Mann, *et celui qui vend les 100,000 chemises partout dans le Métro.*

Henry Miller

During one of his exploratory forays, Miller observed a young prostitute with a wooden leg. From midnight on, she always took up the same position at the entrance to a dark blind alley next to Gaumont Palace, lit by the red light from the nearby *hôtel de passe*. It was doubtless this disabled *fille de joie* who inspired Henry to make this curious remark in *Tropic of Cancer*:

> I have never seen a place like Paris for varieties of sexual provender. As soon as a woman loses a front tooth or an eye or a leg she goes on the loose. In America she'd starve to death if she had nothing to recommend her but a

mutilation. Here it is different. A missing tooth or a nose eaten away or a fallen womb, any misfortune that aggravates the natural homeliness of the female, seems to be regarded as an added spice, a stimulant for the jaded appetites of the male.

And yet he was intrigued by this woman. When she appears earlier in the novel, he muses that it "must be strange taking that wooden stump to bed with you. One imagines all sorts of things — splinters, etc." He notes in *Quiet Days in Clichy* that she has her "faithful little clientele which kept her busy."

Henry also explored the intersection between the Place de Clichy and the Porte de Clichy called "La Fourche." ["Fork" or, alternatively, "crotch." — *Tr.*] La Fourche! A prophetic name if ever there was one! Destiny itself must have placed it in the path of the author of the *Tropics*, and it must have been for his benefit alone that Avenue Clichy branched off from Avenue Saint-Ouen, like two widening thighs. Crotches abound in Miller's work — as in "opening his crotch," "buried his hand in her crotch," and so on. Anyway, it was at this fourche, on a small side street called Le Chapelais, that Miller happened upon a cheap bistro at which he began to take his evening meal. What most attracted him to the place was not so much the cooking, though it was as flavorful as the owner's banter was colorful, but the unassuming little house directly across the street from it — in front of which, all night long, two or three *poules* cast their nets. Miller had a ringside seat and could watch the whole hustling game being played out as he ate. "Well, there it was," he writes in "Vive la France," "food and sex."

Sometimes Henry went as far down as the Saint-Lazare train station to watch prostitutes accost the men, and to see the "thick tide of semen flooding the gutters"(*Tropic of Can-*

cer). At other times he went to the Médrano Circus, whose famous clowns he had always adored. He had been dreaming of this circus, which was so dear to Picasso, since the day a Brooklyn librarian first sang its praises to him. And one of his favorite places in Paris was the cemetery in Montmartre, where, among others, Stendhal and Heine are buried. I put a photograph of it in my *Paris by Night* collection. Henry had this to say about it in "The Eye of Paris": "The Cemetery Montmartre . . . shot from the bridge at night is a phantasmagoric creation of death flowering in electricity; the intense patches of night lie upon the tombs and crosses in a crazy patchwork of steel girders which fade with the sunlight into bright green lawns and flower beds and graveled walks." Henry also loved watching the ghostly evaporation of night, giving way to the first glow of day spreading across the city. Sometimes, to better capture this fleeting moment, he prowled through the night all the way up to Sacré Coeur to catch dawn's arrival on a Paris still shrouded in sleep.

One day, Fred and Henry were visited by Jean Renaud, the young instructor Henry had met in Dijon. He arrived with two bottles of burgundy in his satchel. Since he didn't know Paris, Henry acted as his guide. One can only imagine what kind of Paris he showed the young man! Eiffel Tower, Arc de Triomphe, Invalides, Notre Dame? Not a chance. Miller showed him Ménilmontant, Belleville, Bagnolet, the Buttes-Chaumont, the Saint Martin canal, the slaughterhouses of La Villette — in short, the gamy, grimy, untouristic Paris he loved so.

Certain hilarious and bawdy episodes from these days of "illumination" Miller would later immortalize in *Quiet Days in Clichy*. He himself admits the title was completely misleading. After all, there was all that brouhaha over that Austrian friend of Fred's who had escaped from prison and was being hunted by the police, and whom they hid in

Clichy for two months. And then that wretched business when Fred was accused of corrupting a minor by letting a girl of fourteen who had run away from home stay with them. But the greatest storm of all to wreak itself upon Clichy occurred in the summer of 1932. June suddenly arrived from New York.

IX

June

One evening on Boulevard Raspail, near where the cafés of
Montparnasse are clustered, beneath a streetlight that had
just that second gone on, I spotted Henry in the middle of a
violent argument with a woman. All I could see of the
woman was a large black cape and a cascade of auburn hair.
When I got closer I was overwhelmed by the pungently
sweet smell of perfume.

"Brassaï," Henry said when he saw me. "This is my
wife, June. She's just arrived from New York."

What I saw was a neck as long as a swan's emerging from
a tight black velour dress, a neck out of a Modigliani painting, supporting a wide and striking face with prominent
cheekbones. Beneath green makeup, June's eyes sparkled,
and her full lips, which were very red, stood out against her
pale face. I had never seen a face that pale. It was the color of
coconut milk and rice powder. Baudelaire, who loved the art
and artifice of a woman's face, would have swooned at the
feet of this creature. She looked as if she were straight off a

page of *Fleurs du Mal*. And that voice! Deep, serious, rich, provocative, like Marlene Dietrich's. Henry thought June's voice evoked all the spices of the east: clove, nutmeg, brown sugar. Every time I saw June after that first meeting, she looked as pale and as anemic, and she always wore a suit or a tight black or purple dress, and a long, flowing cape. There was a theatrical air about her — the upward tilt of the head, the suppleness of her rapid stride, the self-assurance. She was sophisticated right down to her finger-tips, but could also play the vamp, and with her eerie beauty, seductive charm, and undeniable power over both men and women, she had all the makings of a femme fatale.

Psychiatrists like to class people in categories, depending on their character and temperament. What they cannot measure is the intensity and sheer voltage of someone's life force. There are people who have ten times, sometimes a hundred times, more of it than others. Goethe called these supercharged creatures "demoniacs," by which he did not mean that they were possessed by the devil, but simply that they were creatures with a superabundance of life, "something which escapes analysis, reason, comprehension." Goethe felt this strange surging power in himself. He also felt he needed to protect himself from it. June was consumed by the same devouring flame. Henry wrote that she loved excess in all things and believed in every kind of orgy — sexual, conversational, sacrificial.

One cannot talk about Miller as a writer without also talking about June. He was thirty when he met her, and felt he needed something to "shake him up." This "something" turned out to be June. Having a wife and a baby daughter didn't stop Miller from going out on the town in New York, and one evening, with seventy-five dollars in his pocket (for perhaps the first time in his entire life) Miller happened into a dance hall on Broadway, lit up by a string of red lights, called the Orpheum Dance Palace. He saw a very pretty taxi dancer heading for him at full tilt, parting the crowd of jazzed-up dancers. It was love at first sight: "It's got me in the guts." He started shaking. He was already jealous when his dance was over and another young man been chosen for the next. He waited in front of a drugstore on Times Square for her to get off work. She arrived. They had an intimate dinner at Chin Lee's, a Chinese restaurant across from the Orpheum. This was no ordinary taxi dancer. She was cultivated. She couldn't stop talking about Strindberg, her idol, and knew every one of his works. In fact, she was "saturated" with Strindberg and passionate about the battle of the sexes. Henry remembered everything about this first conversation, for a Strindbergian theme ran through their life together like a silver wire. "We came together in a dance of death and so quickly was I sucked down into the vortex that when I came to the surface again I could not recognize the world," he remembers in *Tropic of Cancer.* June compared him to Strindberg: "You're as crazy as he is, and you want as badly to be punished!" Miller was in a state of delirium: "One can wait a whole lifetime for a moment like this," he writes in *Tropic of Capricorn.* Sitting right across from him, talking to him, was the woman he had almost given up waiting for.

The week that followed their first meeting was the happiest of Miller's life, and by the time it was over, the woman had already changed his life's direction. A year later he divorced Beatrice Sylvas and married June. She had total confidence and unshakable faith in Miller's talents as a writer — though there was nothing to justify it — and made him quit his demeaning job at Western Union. "My only reason for living," she would tell him, "is to see you do what you want to do. Trust me. I know what's best for you.

You must write... Don't worry... We'll get through it... Leave it to me." For seven years she was his oracle and his muse.

As it turned out, of course, even June's care and devotion weren't enough to spark a creative flame, and the years went by with only sterile literary exercises to show for them. It would take a second, and even more violent, shock to set Miller to writing.

June worked as a B-girl at a gay nightclub for both sexes in Greenwich Village, and was courted by some of the butchest lesbians around. She herself preferred seraphic-looking women and, one evening, fell madly in love with a young Russian woman whom Miller would call "Anastasia." So powerful was this sudden crush that June brought Anastasia home that very night to the dark basement apartment she shared with Henry. His pride was wounded deeply, and his virility humiliated. What would their friends say? He was convinced they would think there was something wrong with him. For Henry anyway, things began to deteriorate from there. The lovebirds, engrossed in each other, completely ignored him, leaving him for hours without money, light, or heating. Famished, feeling like a prisoner sitting in his cell in chains, he waited up for them every night. As soon as they returned, hand in hand, in the small hours of the morning, Henry pounced like some wild animal on the food they brought. Sometimes they asked him to leave them for a while; they wanted to entertain a "friend" or a "benefactor," a bearer of food, gifts, or checks. For Henry it was total defeat. June and "Stasia," meanwhile, conspired. Henry wondered if they were planning to run away, for he knew that they dreamed of Paris and of Montparnasse. Sure enough, one day Miller came home to find a note from June. She and Stasia had embarked for Europe on the *Rochambeau*. "I didn't have the courage to tell you," the note read. "Write to me care of American Express in Paris. Kisses." Miller groaned "like a grenadier with a mortal wound." Then he started to scream at the top of his lungs. Pent-up jealousy and resentment came pouring out.

For some time there was no news from June. Finally a letter arrived. Having separated from Anastasia, June had gone to Vienna "with some friends," she wrote. Henry knew very well that these friends were idle and wealthy young Americans willing to squire June around. In the meantime, in order to survive, Henry had taken a job at the Queen's County municipal cemetery, and it was there — caught up in dark despair but also in complete possession of his abilities — that at five one afternoon, he began to sketch out his novel about his love for June, which would become *The Rosy Crucifixion*. "The truth is I wrote this dread book in my head when jotting down (in the space of about eighteen continuous hours) the complete outline or notes covering the subject matter of this work. I made this cryptic skeleton of the magnum opus during a period of brief separation — from 'Her,' " he wrote in his essay on H. Rider Haggard's *She*. At the time Henry was sketching the book out, he was obsessing over the years he had spent with June, whom he wanted both to immortalize and to destroy. But this work, too, he kept putting off and putting off, and didn't actually start the "magnum opus" until thirteen years later, only to drop it again and again.

One wonders whether June knew that Henry needed to be shaken up in order to fly with his own wings. It seems likely. Without her treason, he never would have found his artistic freedom. She was the one who got the inner Henry Miller moving. Miller saw no way of easing his misery other than by elaborating loud and long on the highs and lows of their love, and making the whole world a witness to the injustice and humiliation. He felt that he had been wounded like no man before him had ever been wounded, and that his work was born of his martyrdom. He wrote in *Tropic of Capricorn*, "It was more painful than anything I had ever experienced before, but it was also healing." Interestingly, in *Time Refound*, Marcel Proust also attested to the necessity of betrayal to the creative artist: "The resentment of an affront, the agonies of abandonment — these would have been territory we would never have known, and the discovery of which, painful as it is to men, becomes something precious to the artist."

★   ★   ★

Henry's passion for June, the "queen mother of all the slippery Babylonian whores," as he describes her in *Tropic of Capricorn*, always reminds me of the passion the knight Des Grieux feels for Manon Lescaut — as stormy, as violent, and as fatal. It was the perfidious nature of woman, her elusiveness and inconstancy, and the jealousy that nature constantly stirs up within the lover's breast that gives the Abbé Prévost's novel its matchless power, and makes it one of the few out of the so many of this genre to survive. Passionate love, love capable of any crime, made its literary debut in *Manon Lescaut*. I find the parallels between the characters in that novel and in Miller's work striking, even disturbing.

A curious detail: Lencki Eckhardt, Abbé Prévost's mistress and the model for Manon, was herself Hungarian or Romanian originally — born, like June, somewhere in Carpathia. Observing Manon's arrival by carriage from Amiens, the knight Des Grieux feels the same thunderbolt of love that had struck Miller in that Broadway dance hall — "In one second I was deliriously inflamed" — and also the same feeling of fatality: "Fatal passion! Whether living in Europe or in America, why would I care if I were sure I'd be happy living there with my mistress!" And then Miller in *Sexus:* "Mara, Mara, where are you leading me? It's fateful, it's ominous, but I belong to you body and soul, and you will take me where you will, deliver me to my keeper, bruised, crushed, broken." You can hear the voice of the knight speaking with all the ardor of the eighteenth century when Henry writes that they were joined by their loins. Slightly more discreet, Des Grieux talks of "delirious pleasure," and countless caresses.

Manon and her lover open a honkytonk in The Hague; Henry and June opened a speakeasy in Greenwich Village, right in the middle of Prohibition. Like the knight, Henry simultaneously performed the duties of manager, bartender, cashier, delivery boy, and secretary. Like Manon, June was attracted to the innumerable "benefactors," "friends," and "old crazies" that came in. Sometimes she wanted to be alone with one of them, and sent Henry out on an errand. When he got back, she took several minutes to open the door to him, or would even beg him to come back an hour later. So too did Manon make Des Grieux wait for her outside the door of her boudoir. Both men couldn't help noticing the improvement in the quality of life and the "apparent increase in opulence" (Des Grieux). Where was the money coming from? When the knight pressed Manon on the subject, she laughingly replied that he shouldn't worry his head about it; she would always find something. June would also return home early in the morning, her arms filled with goodies — champagne, caviar, presents of all sorts. If Henry tried to find out where they came from, she would shrug and tell him not to ask so many questions. Wherever they went, June and Manon, seductresses both, were instantly surrounded by shadowy figures or getting secret messages. June would no sooner meet Henry in a café than she would disappear to use the phone, or to send a *pneumatique*[1] or a telegram.

At bottom, like Des Grieux, Henry always preferred uncertainty, vagueness, and doubt, and never pushed his investigations too far. His friends took these things to heart more than he did. They told Miller he was a romantic, and that he preferred mystery to honesty. Miller's indifference was affected, however, and disguised (badly, sometimes) his scorn and his jealousy. He unburdened his heart when he wrote, such as when he describes the tribulations of a Parisian pimp in *Tropic of Cancer*:

> A pimp has his private grief and misery too, don't you forget . . . Perhaps it isn't so wonderful, when he bends over his Lucienne, to taste another man's breath . . . Bet you, when she squeezes him tight, when she begs for that little package of love which only he knows how to deliver, bet you he fights like a thousand devils to pump it up, to wipe out that regiment that has marched between her legs.

When their mistresses' infidelities became too obvious to ignore, the two lovers were "mortally wounded." Miller felt "crucified"; Des Grieux was the "unhappiest, the most unfortunate of all creatures." Their passion vacillated between joy and misery. "My feelings perpetually alternated between hate and love, hope and despair, depending on which image of Manon came to mind." She could be "the most lovable of all girls" one moment, and the next a "wretched liar" and "a weak and perfidious mistress." Henry

---

[1] Translator's note: One of the easiest and most popular ways of sending messages around Paris at the time was by means of the tubes connecting the PTT, or post office, in one *arrondissement* to the others. Notes were put into containers and pushed through the tubes by the creation of a partial vacuum, the same principle as a vacuum cleaner. Once they arrived at the PTT nearest to the addressee, they were then hand-delivered.

and June also argued like mad, going from horrible rupture to tender rapture and back again. For Miller and for Des Grieux, agony and ecstasy were interwoven. A thousand times they would swear to leave their mistresses, but so strong was the women's charm that their presence alone was powerful enough to soften steely convictions and force their will to bend. Des Grieux begged Manon to forgive him, and Miller always gave in to "absolute capitulation." Love transmuted everything: faults became virtues; betrayals, acts of pure devotion; lies and dissembling, shining examples of discretion and delicacy of feeling. In the last analysis, vanity prevailed. The two cuckolds delighted that of all the aspirants — though they were younger, more handsome, and wealthier — *they* were the chosen ones. Far from doing harm to Manon for seducing so many young men, her knight-servant is thrilled to be loved by someone whom so many admire and want to possess. The same for Henry, as we see in this passage from *Sexus:* "My ideal — it gave me quite a shock to formulate it! — was that of a woman who had the world at her feet. If I thought there were men impervious to her charms I would deliberately aid her to ensnare them. The more lovers she garnered the greater my own personal triumph. Because she did love *me*, that there was no doubt about. Had she not singled me out from all the others, I, who had so little to offer her?" From the pitiful "beaten dog" he becomes the "frisky top dog," the "thing" to Mona. He suddenly couldn't give a damn how many other men there were in her life, just so long as he was a "link in the chain." And when she comes home with her arms full, her cheeks rosy, and her eyes shining, he is happy — because she is happy.

★　　　★　　　★

Passive, accommodating women were of no interest to Miller. "Good girls" and "shrinking violets" were not his type.

He wouldn't be taken in by anyone lacking in mystery, however beautiful she might be. "I am immune to this kind of woman," he once told me. "After a few weeks, I get completely bored." He loved women who were hard to pin down, unreachable, impenetrable. By those standards he couldn't have done better than June, who was an enigma from first day to last. No one could resist her — neither man nor woman. A "live volcano," a "female Vesuvius," even her body was in constant metamorphosis. A born egomaniac and actress, June was slithery as an eel. Her identity kept slipping between his fingers and what he knew about her life was a dissimulation, the truth mysterious and secret. Her background, her birthplace, even her true name were unknown to him. But from the moment they first met in that dance hall, Henry was enthralled. He married her without really knowing whom he was marrying — was she June Mansfield? Edith Smith? Klotilde? Mara? Mona?

In Henry's eyes, June's mysteriousness transformed her straight into myth. She was like Helen or Juno. She was like Ayesha in H. Rider Haggard's *She*, another unearthly creature of immortal beauty whose charm no one could resist. In fact, June *was* Ayesha. He wondered if she too would be consumed by the flames of life, drawn there by her beauty and allure, which endowed her with power that bordered on sorcery. June was "a bottomless abyss, impenetrable," and even after Henry's decade-long, Strindbergian dance of death with her, she was still no more accessible than an "ice sculpture" sitting in the garden of some forgotten continent. Everything June did was shrouded in secrecy. She spent her days inventing, embroidering, plotting, and finally believing in her own stories. Her words were ambiguous, her replies evasive. Henry tried to fight back, but became lost in a labyrinth of lies. June was like those Orientals whose art is predicated on the notion of concealment.

In 1932, during his short stay in Dijon, Miller read Proust's *The Prisoner* and *Albertine Disappeared*, and was enraptured by them. It was clear to him that Marcel had had to fight the same tissue of lies, from Albertine, and to endure the same inextinguishable jealousy that he did. These books set his mind to spinning. He could hardly resist underlining every word, for everything he read about Albertine reminded him of June. He was fascinated. He felt Proust must have written them for him alone.[2]

★   ★   ★

Miller often talked of June, of her great beauty, her enormous powers of seduction, and her wonderful body, and however much Parisian life preoccupied and enchanted him, he could never escape her image. He wondered if the day would come when she would be back in his arms again. The narrow backstreets, the banks of the Seine, the out-of-the-way nooks where there were a few benches and plane trees, the bistros — every corner of Paris had borne witness to their love, and to their rending scenes of jealousy. Everything reminded Henry of June, and embellished her memory. After all, she had been the one who had told him that he had to go to Paris and become a writer. She had also told him that he must go alone, that she would join him there later. And so they had parted. "When I realize that she is gone," he

---

2 Another work about jealousy that made a strong impression on Miller was *Le Cocu magnifique* (*The Magnificent Cuckold*): "I knew the author, Fernand Crommelynck," he once told me. "One day someone introduced me to this Flemish writer at the Dôme. Alas, I only read his book twenty years later and I was fascinated by it! I adore the Flemish spirit. How many times have I regretted that I couldn't tell Crommelynck how much I thought of his book. I think it one of the most beautiful things ever written about jealousy. I would even put it over Shakespeare's *Othello*." — *Au.*

writes in *Tropic of Cancer*, "perhaps gone forever, a great void opens up and I feel that I am falling, falling, falling into deep, black space."

And then came that day when June suddenly announced she was in France. She had scraped together enough money to live in Paris for a time. One might have expected Henry to be elated, but the news made him frantic, even traumatized him. He feared June as much as he desired her. Their love might be in ashes, but the smallest puff of wind could reignite it. More than June's "traps," Henry feared his own weakness, his tendency toward "unconditional surrender" in her magnetic presence. Sex and all the senses it had heightened had created an indissoluble bond between them. Yet he knew that if she came back to him, the chaos would begin again and he would become lost in it. His life as a professional writer in Paris was finally beginning. He was forty years old and hadn't a minute to spare. June's arrival meant that all his plans would crumble like a house of cards. He prepared himself to do whatever was necessary to finish his *Tropic* and all the other books that were coming to a boil. He would protect those works as a mother would protect her young. Four years earlier, after June's desertion, passing in front of the Orpheum Dance Palace on Broadway, it wasn't of June that he was thinking, but of his unborn book. June-Mara-Mona had become a protagonist in his novel rather than a woman in his life. "It came over me, as I stood there, that I wasn't thinking of her any more; I was thinking of this book which I am writing, and the book had become more important to me than her, than all that had happened to us" (*Tropic of Capricorn*).

The painter Pierre Bonnard expressed very well this sort of conflict between the painter's original inspiration and the "double," as it were, taking shape on the canvas. "The presence of the subject can be very unhealthy for the painter," he wrote in the journal *Verve*. "The starting point is an idea and if the subject is there at the moment the artist begins work, there is the danger that he will allow himself to be distracted by actual, immediate life. The painter will no longer be able to find his starting point again and ally himself with the incidental." Miller also feared that June's sudden intrusion would erase the image of Mona, as she had by now taken shape in his mind. He feared he would lose control over the original vision and, in June's presence, allow himself to get taken in by the "incidental" and in "actual, immediate life."

That was why, when June stepped off the train in Saint-Lazare, Henry begged her to leave him alone. June couldn't understand, and there were bitter fights, another paroxysm of their dance of death. Shaking with sobs, swept up in an orgy of hysterical crying, she accused Henry of being an ingrate, a heartless beast, a monster.

Henry complained bitterly about all this to me. After June's arrival in Paris he had stopped working altogether, and I had never seen him so agitated and anxious. His attempts to escape had failed. He hadn't found a way to break June's velvet grip. He thought his manuscripts might be in danger. Countless pages of notes that were to become *Tropic of Capricorn* were stacked in his desk drawers, and he feared that if June read them and became enraged she might do anything — tear them to shreds or burn them, annihilating the fruit of many months of work.

★　　★　　★

In his despair, Henry begged Anaïs to save him from this fury. Intense curiosity, mixed with jealousy and animosity, drew these two women to each other. June cast a sinister eye at this moneyed, bourgeois woman who had supplanted her — on the intellectual and material level, at least — in Miller's heart. And Anaïs couldn't repress her feelings of jealousy mixed with admiration, and perhaps envy, for this long-standing object of Miller's passion. Still, Anaïs became the arbiter in the daily quarrels into which June and Henry threw themselves. Pulled one way and then the other, she wondered how long she could keep playing her part when, as if scripted, dramatic resolution presented itself.

From everything Henry had told her or written her, Anaïs had expected June to be a frivolous woman, a thoroughgoing, cruel vamp. She discovered to her surprise that June was a romantic figure, tender and loyal-hearted, who thought only of Miller's well-being, and who was ready to sacrifice herself for the one true love of her life. June's bewitching charm caused Anaïs to revise Henry's unforgiving portrait. He saw June as lost in a labyrinth of lies; Anaïs sympathized with her constant need to surround herself with dreams and marvels. June was like André Breton's Nadja, because, like Nadja, June was a creative spirit who could transform daily reality into magic. She had the same preternatural acuity and prophetic gifts Breton had admired in Nadja, "one of these spirits of the air who can bestow favor without ever compromising themselves." I can't help wondering if Breton would have spoken of Nadja with as much lyricism had he had to live under the same roof with her, year after year, as Henry had with June. In any case, Anaïs's feelings toward this touching victim of egoism softened and, little by little, awoke in her a nascent attraction for her own sex, a penchant she had already revealed in several passages of her *Diary*. In short, Anaïs fell madly in love with June.

We can't know how intimate they actually became, and whether Anaïs really loved June with a love that went beyond the platonic. But it is a fact that Anaïs was swept off her feet. Arm in arm, the two women went out to nightclubs and danced together, kissing each other on the lips. Years later, in November 1937, Anaïs still thought of June when she went to visit a lesbian couple. The sight of their reciprocated love revived memories of June. The younger woman of the pair, with her face framed by angelic hair, with her voluptuous body, raspy voice, strong arms, and slightly feverish look, was June's twin. She was stretched out on her bed, her half-open negligee revealing the bronze skin of her thighs and exposing her breasts, on which her friend was lying. Anaïs couldn't take her eyes off them all afternoon. Perhaps she was remembering what had happened, or not happened, between herself and June.

It is also possible that by loving June, Anaïs, who burned with the desire to try everything, was only striving to share Henry's passion for the "love of his life." Besides, did June really love Anaïs? Rejected and abandoned by Henry, June might only have been thinking of depriving him, out of spite, of the woman whose moral and material support was now more than ever indispensable to him. Whatever the case, for a time the two women were in league against Henry. It was the last skirmish in the Strindbergian war of the sexes.

★　　　★　　　★

Time to move to the last chapter on this grand love. Penniless and threatened with eviction from her Montparnasse hotel, June asked Henry for money. She was, after all, his wife. He too was broke, as always, but he also didn't attempt to find any for her. "And to do her justice," he writes in "Via Dieppe-Newhaven," which contains his reminiscences of their last days together, "I must add that had the situation been reversed the money would have been forthcoming; she always knew how to raise money for me but never for herself. That I've got to admit." "I felt like a louse," Miller added. He did find the money finally (Anaïs gave it to him), but instead of rushing over to Montparnasse to help June out, he immediately planned a trip to London. "After turning round and round like a rat in a trap I got the brilliant idea of beating it myself. Just walk out on the problem, that's always the easiest way." His little scheme fell apart when June came out to Clichy the night before he was to leave. There was screaming. Tears. Hugs. Kisses. Hysteria. Worn down by it all, Miller relented, having "got to the point of guilt and tenderness," and confessed to June that he had planned to run off with the money. He took it out of his pocket and placed it on the table. June took it.

Henry had already bought his ticket to London and decided to go anyway. But when he got to Newhaven without so much as a penny in his pocket, the British authorities refused him entry. Henry panicked. What would happen if the French police didn't let him back into France? His greatest fear, he once told Anaïs, was being forced to bounce from one country to another like a vagabond. The French border guards treated him leniently, however, and he returned without incident to Paris. Henry was deeply moved by this. "Yes, as the train rolled out of the station I distinctly remember two big tears rolling down my cheeks and falling on to my hands. I felt safe again and among human beings." June, for her part, returned to New York. Their marriage dissolved three years later.

Henry's account of their final moments together in "Via Dieppe-Newhaven" is haunting: "She said good-bye and she stood there on the stairs looking up at me with a strange sorrowful smile. If I had made the least gesture I know she would have thrown the money out of the window and rushed back into my arms and stayed with me forever. I took a long look at her, walked slowly back to the door, and closed it. I went back to the kitchen table, sat there a few minutes looking at the empty glasses, and then I broke down and sobbed like a child."

So much for quiet days in Clichy!

X

Villa Seurat

In the autumn of 1934 the Clichy adventure came to an end, having lasted for just two years. Anaïs wanted Henry to move back to Paris proper, and the idea of his living in the Villa Seurat had long preoccupied her. That summer she visited this elegant little cul-de-sac located in the 14th arrondissement, between Montparnasse and Montsouris Park, and consisting of twenty small art-deco houses — each one painted a different color — and rented an apartment for Henry. Rents were high, out of the reach of everyone except well-heeled foreigners, diplomats, businessmen, and artists who had "arrived," such as Chagall, Lurçat, Dali, and Soutine. The affluent denizens of this popular hangout gave big parties with music, flowers, plentiful whiskey, bathtubs filled with punch. The one artist who never joined in the festivities was Chaim Soutine, who never invited anyone in, even his oldest friends.

Henry's address was 18 Villa Seurat, a comfortable, light, and cheerful arrangement consisting of a studio, a small bedroom, a bathroom, a loggia, a skylight, and a minuscule kitchen set up in a closet. Four years earlier, during his "bum" period, he had stayed in the same house, because Michael Fraenkel, known in the *Tropic of Cancer* as "Boris," lived on the ground floor. Miller gradually incorporated the Villa Seurat into his work, into his very notion of France. When he revisited this sanctuary thirty years later, at the age of seventy-five, he found it a sad, soulless little street with rundown houses. Henry wondered why he had found it so irresistible.

To their friends, it came as a great surprise that the seemingly inseparable Henry and Fred were now separated. Their cohabitation had obviously had its advantages, but it had also had its disadvantages, and these latter had become too much for Henry. He needed elbow room. His bosom buddy had become a little too indiscreet, was a little too much in love with "Pietà," the name he'd given Anaïs. "Henry is wild with happiness," she noted in her *Diary*. "Fred is hurt because he wasn't invited to go and live in the Villa Seurat. But Henry wants to be alone." That is not exactly how things happened. Fred was living in the apartment when Miller suddenly threw him out. And Perlès was more than just "hurt" — he was traumatized. What made matters worse was that he had just lost his job at the *Chicago Herald Tribune*, which had been teetering for some time and now closed down completely.

He wrote me a dramatic letter in September 1934 to tell me about the reversal of his fortunes:

My dear friend,

I am so sorry, so apologetic, disappointed. I have just now been asked to leave the Villa Seurat, and this means I will have to cancel our rendezvous for tomorrow night. It all happened very suddenly and I didn't see it coming. I have to be out this very morning. I don't know yet where I'll go, especially since I'm broke . . . and can't give you a forwarding address, not having one. All this has arrived at the worst possible time.

Perlès's first novel, *Sentiments limitrophes,* was about to appear and he was busy correcting the proofs, as well as organizing his own promotion and publicity campaigns.

Henry asked his friend Roger Klein if he would take Fred in. Though Klein's studio on Rue des Artistes, near Montsouris Park, was very small, and he lived there with his wife Maguy, he generously agreed. "I couldn't just leave him on the sidewalk," Roger told me.

He looked like a beaten spaniel, with those careworn, tormented eyes of his, and I felt sorry for him. But do you remember? The dominant feature of his character was to pile up as many female conquests as possible, as if their sheer number would raise his esteem in their eyes. He preferred the wives of his friends, especially. He warned me with provocative honesty. 'Watch out, Roger! I might stab you in the back. It's in my nature.' Not long after, I had to go to the country, and when I got back I discovered that Fred had indeed tried to do what he warned me about. With neither anger nor regret, I threw him out. He wasn't that important to me.

Henry was not unaware of Fred's character flaw when he asked Roger to house him. Of Fred, he wrote that if he wanted to sleep with a girl, he'd do it, "even if it meant spitting on a friend."

Slowly, Fred's life quieted down. He found a job and a small apartment in the same cul-de-sac where lived the painter Hans Reichel and the "occultist" David Edgar, both friends. And before too long, he was back at the Villa Seurat revisiting his "Pietà" and her god as if nothing had happened. Their separation was not a divorce, it was simply physical and material, and Henry could note that even though officially they were leading separate lives, they were still always together.

By a strange coincidence, *Tropic of Cancer* appeared at the end of September 1934, the same day Miller moved into the Villa Seurat, where, four years earlier, he had first begun working on the book. His publisher, Jack Kahane, brought him the first copy, with its odd-looking black and green dust jacket, featuring a giant crab devouring a naked woman. Miller enthusiastically signed copies of his book, and Anaïs packed them up, glued on the address labels, and licked the stamps. She also sent out hundreds of flyers and wrote piles of letters to her friends. It was a memorable day in Henry's life. "The publication of a book," the poet Pierre Reverdy once told me, "is something truly moving." How else could it feel to a forty-three-year-old author, holding in his hand at long last his first offspring. He was so mad with joy he nearly had a cerebral hemorrhage. Walking back to my hotel on Rue de la Glacière on the evening of September 23, 1934, I found a copy of *Tropic* sitting in my mailbox. On the title page was written, "To my dear friend Halasz, Henry V. Miller." A small note was enclosed: "Here's the book! Finally! I'm now living at 18 Villa Seurat, first floor, on the left. (You'll see a painting on the door). As ever, Henry V. Miller."

From that point onward and for several years, we were nearly neighbors. Sometimes we'd have dinner together. Here is one of his notes to me, written in 1934 or 1935: "My dear Halasz — come on Friday around 7 to dinner. And bring your camera. Anaïs would like some pictures taken of her in costume." At the time, Anaïs was taking dance lessons and thinking seriously about becoming a professional dancer. I remember her very well on that occasion — her face was as pale and transparent as alabaster, and her large, moist eyes conveyed deep sadness. I photographed her dressed as a Spanish dancer and swathed in romantic veils, while Henry, the grand chef, was making dinner. "Dear Halasz, the photo in the Hindu shawl is a great success," Anaïs wrote me, asking if I would send her several copies of it so that she could take them to New York. It was about this time that she wrote in her *Diary:* "Brassaï is never without his camera. He has prominent eyes, as if he had spent too much time looking through a camera lens. He doesn't look like he's observant, but as soon as his attention is caught by a person or thing, it's as if he becomes hypnotized. He goes on talking to you without looking at you."

Tropic of Cancer had a painful birth. Henry had begun writing it during his vagabond stage, burdened by the feeling that he needed to make up for lost time. "My one consolation," he told me one day, "is that Cervantes, Jean-Jacques Rousseau, and Marcel Proust were all older than me when they got going." He didn't want to let a single day go by without writing. He knew right from the start that he would avoid writing pure fiction. The only form that could express the vehemence of his savage mood was autobiography. But — how and where to start? He was saturated with source material (of which not even a tenth would ever be used), but the subject that was closest to his heart was his seven-year dance of death with June. After that came his childhood in Brooklyn. Could he simply ignore the very recent past, and the present, meaning his nomadic life in Paris? Of course he couldn't. For one thing, each page of the manuscript was written in a different place — at Fraenkel's, Fred's, Osborn's, or beneath the lights of a Clichy café. He could fill up five or ten pages at a sitting, each one a furious digression with neither form nor order nor narrative thread.

The only thing tying these picaresque adventures together was the personality of the narrator himself, who could be, by turns, playful, sentimental, despairing, joyful, tragic, aggressive, or obscene. While he was writing his work, he had the sensation of being pregnant: "I walk through the streets big with child and the cops escort me across the street. Women get up to offer me their seats" (*Tropic of Cancer*). All the drifting around could sometimes exasperate him, and there were times when he lost heart, but this wandering life did not do damage to his writing. The book was written, as he tells Anaïs in a letter dated April 26, 1934, "on the wing, as it were, between my 25 addresses. It gives the sensation of constant change of address, environment, etc. Like a bad dream. And for that it is good. Hectic. Kaleidoscopic."

Not only was the original manuscript good, hectic, and kaleidoscopic, it was also unpublishable. Henry had given free rein to a furious unraveling of passions — erotic scenes and obscene stories that no publisher, neither in France nor elsewhere, would dare to print. Even Anaïs, who recognized the mark of Henry's genius, grumbled about certain passages she found particularly crude. Refusing categorically to edit out these passages, Henry attempted to justify himself. He was trying to write as a man, and to be true to his art he could suppress nothing. Henry and Anaïs would fail to find a publisher.

Through the intermediary of the literary agent and writer William A. Bradley, Henry was introduced to Jack Kahane, who was British, a former textile manufacturer, and a devotee of erotic literature. Kahane had himself written some licentious novels and published them under a pseudonym. The Obelisk Press, the house Kahane had founded in Paris, published only English-language books — including his own — and took on books that had been banned in America or England, such as Frank Harris's *My Life and*

Loves. Kahane read and loved *Tropic of Cancer*. He said it was more powerful than *Lady Chatterley's Lover* or *Ulysses*, and he would tell anyone who'd listen that it would be the book of the century. Others who read Miller's manuscript confirmed his assessment, and word spread that the unknown man in the rumpled overcoat was nothing less than a genius. A contract was drawn up and signed. Kahane promised Henry heaven and earth. He even said he would publish a French edition simultaneously. I remember Henry's face when he told me the news one evening in Montparnasse. The French edition turned out to be a pipe dream, alas. The contract stipulated that Henry would get a fixed royalty of ten percent on copies sold for fifty francs — the price of three dinners — and not one penny in advance. As before, he would simply have to live hand to mouth. Miller thought that was too bad, but resigned himself to it. What was most important was that the book get published.

It didn't, not immediately. There were delays, mostly owing to more repercussions of the 1929 crash: bank closings, moratoriums, bankruptcy, currency devaluations. Nearly ruined financially, and fearing that no one would buy *Tropic of Cancer*, Kahane asked Miller for a six-month extension on publishing the book, and then after six months he begged for other extensions. Miller was in despair. He thought that if *Tropic* didn't appear right away, it never would. Finally, exasperated by Kahane's delays, Anaïs decided in May of 1934 — *in extremis* — to give Obelisk Press enough money to cover the cost of the printing.

Financial reasons weren't the only ones behind Kahane's delays; he was also worried about censorship. The French translation of *Lady Chatterley's Lover* was nearly banned, and Miller himself suspected that his novel would cause a storm. To many, his child, his *enfant terrible*, would seem like a monster, a pervert, a juvenile delinquent, a candidate for the insane asylum — a criminal who should be sentenced to prison and carted off. Each time he passed by the statue of Etienne Dolet — Rabelais's printer and the publisher of *Pantagruel* — on Boulevard Saint-Germain, Miller reflected on the woes that might befall Jack Kahane. Dolet was hanged and burned for spreading subversive ideas. Showing his stiff, British upper lip, Kahane told Miller that they would go to prison together.

The two-year delay was filled with disappointments, but one happy result was that the novel was completely reworked. With her able judgment, and her sense of structure and pacing, Anaïs helped Miller edit out some of the overwritten passages. She suggested that the sequence of the chapters be changed, and was merciless about what she termed Henry's "childish extravagances," wanting to prevent him from making the same mistakes that she felt Lawrence had made in *Lady Chatterley's Lover.* She thought the novel should be reduced from six hundred pages to three hundred. This was too much for Henry to bear. He reacted as if she had cut into his own flesh, fiercely defending every word, every sentence, every page. Still, all the postponements meant he was able to spin out three or four versions, of which the last is incontestably the best. The same thing had happened to Proust, though with completely different results. In the beginning, *Remembrance of Things Past* was to consist of three volumes: *Swann's Way, The Guermantes Way,* and *Time Refound.* The outbreak of war in 1914 halted publication, and six years of reprieve allowed the work to grow new branches — *Sodom and Gomorrah, The Prisoner, Albertine Disappeared* — and to assume proportions even the author hadn't foreseen.

The delays had another advantage, in that they gave Miller time to discover Céline's *Journey to the End of Night,* a work to which he later openly confessed his indebtedness.

Céline's writing electrified him, inspiring him to try to inject the reviving serum of spoken language into his own prose. What connections there are between Céline and Miller! The American part of *Journey* must have reminded Henry of his days at Western Union. But Céline's bitterness and pessimism — the diagnosis of a suburban doctor who focuses on humanity's scabs, tumors, fevers, and ulcers — contrast with Miller's exuberant optimism. One writer viewed the world through dark glasses, the other through rose-colored ones. Where Miller loved the body and its functions, Céline was horrified by the "shameful" cult of organs and viscera: "the most ridiculous of our servitudes, the most pitiful of our wastes." He was pained that man was guided by his "lower parts" instead of by his dreams and mystic propensities. And while, for Miller, the cult of wine represented the very quintessence of France, all Céline saw was cirrhosis of the liver, delirium tremens, insane asylums, hospital beds, and retarded children. "France has completely sold itself out," he wrote in *Bagatelles for a Massacre*, "liver, nerves, brain, and kidneys, to the big wine producers." "Wine is the national poison!" If gastronomy, French cuisine, wonderful spreads, the variety of cheeses, the pleasures of the main course, and the huge number of restaurants and bistros all represented, in Miller's eyes, refinements in the art of *savoir-vivre* and perhaps the only joys that life afforded, they made Céline vomit. What he saw was bloat, obesity, misery, ravaged youth, and premature old age. He railed tirelessly against the despicable gluttony of the French, whom he accused of eating and drinking ten times what was necessary.

At least they shared common ground when it came to love. Like Miller, Céline preferred the raptures of the flesh to the raptures of the heart. "Ah, Ferdinand," he writes in *The Church*, "so long as you shall live, you will move between

110

the thighs of women to seek the secret of the world." "Her body was for an endless joy. I couldn't get enough of that American body. To be quite honest, I was a complete pig. And I will remain one" (*Journey to the End of Night*).

Like Miller, Céline had been left to his own devices when very young. Self-taught, he traveled widely in order to escape early the stifling atmosphere of family life. Both Miller and Céline were displaced and in contant rebellion against society, which they denounced as despotic and chaotic. Their accumulated rancor and humiliations pushed them into writing literary bombshells that detonated at nearly the same moment. Céline's youth had been spent in a Choiseul alley, Miller's in a poor section of Brooklyn. However, where Henry remembered with tenderness the crumbling plaster, the empty lots, the stench from the factories and steel mills, Céline remembered with disgust the gas pipes and furnace heat of his airless enclosure. To him, Paris would never be anything more than a fetid Choiseul alley, albeit a thousand times bigger, but just as fenced in and putrid. Miller loved Paris for its ambiance and the beauty of its streets; Céline saw only its filth. Of all cities, it was the most "infected and enclosed," a dead end "teeming with cadavers and millions of latrines," a "mountain of filth, a physiological catastrophe." Curious it is that the city Céline most loved was the one Miller most hated, New York, about which Henry writes in *Tropic of Cancer*: "When I think of this city where I was born and raised, this Manhattan that Whitman sang of, a blind, white rage licks my guts. New York! The white prisons, the sidewalks swarming with maggots, the breadlines, the opium joints that are built like palaces, the kikes that are there, the lepers, the thugs, and above all, the *ennui*, the monotony of faces, streets, legs, houses, skyscrapers, meals, posters, jobs, crimes, loves . . ." Céline loved New York for the stimulating ocean air. Paris, being so far from the ocean, stewed in an asphyxiating basin of its own sewage.

★　　★　　★

A small dialogue on the subject of the relationship between Céline and Miller:

> FRANK DOBO: One day I went to see Denoël, one of the directors of a young but dynamic and ambitious publishing house. He said to me: "I have just discovered a masterpiece! Its author is clearly a genius. The other day, someone left an enormous manuscript [*Journey to the End of Night*] on my desk and it intrigued me. I decided to take it with me and began to leaf through it on the way home from the theater. I was immediately enthralled . . . couldn't take my eyes off it. I read through the night. It's a fantastic, stupefying novel, written in a style that owes nothing to anybody, and is so direct and alive that it makes all the others seem wilted and insipid . . . It's not even a novel, but a bludgeon, an explosive, a bomb . . ." Then Denoël told me he'd stayed up for three nights reading it . . . "Right up to the end," he told me, "my interest and enthusiasm never flagged . . ." When I read it myself I was also overwhelmed and showed it to a few friends, including Henry Miller . . . The story behind the manuscript itself is almost like a detective novel.

> ME: It's true, isn't it, that no one knew the name of the author? They asked some employees and learned that a woman had brought it in.

> DOBO: Yes, but it wasn't the novelist's cleaning lady, as some people have believed, it was an American friend of Céline's, the dancer Elisabeth Craig. *Journey* is dedicated

to her. Having found out his name and address, they discovered the author's identity: a doctor named Destouches, whose *nom de plume* was Céline.[1]

ME: Did you ever meet him?

DOBO: Of course. The first time I met him was at his publisher's, on a small street near the Ecole Militaire and the Invalides called Rue Amélie. After that, Céline came to my office fairly often because he was interested in selling foreign rights to his work.

ME: And Miller?

DOBO: I had several clean proofs of *Journey,* and gave him one, so he read it well before its publication. He was bowled over. I had only known Miller for a few months, having met him at a party. I discovered him glued to the buffet table, eating and drinking everything in reach, literally creating a *tabula rasa.* Henry felt a fraternal bond with Céline and believed the connection between *Journey* and his own novel was significant.

ME: Did Henry ever meet Céline?

DOBO: No, alas, he didn't. Still, thinking that being introduced to the author of the novel might make Miller happy, I did everything I could to arrange a meeting. But Céline was very suspicious, even misanthropic. Above all he hated intellectuals, the "men of letters" and *tutti quanti* ... I couldn't persuade him that Miller was not the literati type he hated so much. He had a persecution

---

[1] I later learned that the woman who delivered the manuscript to Denoël was neither his cleaning lady nor Elisabeth Craig, but a woman who lived in the same building as Céline. She was herself a writer, and also dropped off one of her works, and that was how they were able to track Céline down. — *Au.*

complex. He thought everyone was out to get him, to steal from him and take advantage of him. Especially his publisher and his literary agent! Despite all my efforts, a Céline-Miller meeting never took place. Don't forget that to Céline Henry was a complete unknown — *Tropic of Cancer* didn't come out until two years after *Journey*.

ME: Why didn't you show Céline the manuscript of *Tropic*?

DOBO: There were no copies around. After it was published I sent him a copy. His English is extremely good and he read it . . . and thought highly of it. He never elaborated very much. There was someone whom Céline wanted very much to meet, and that was the painter Oskar Kokoschka, who was living in Paris at the time. Do you remember?

ME: I was very close to Kokoschka. He often invited me to his studio near Montsouris Park. I also took lots of photographs when I went there. He was a charming man, full of life . . .

DOBO: Well, Kokoschka had read *Journey* and was so taken with it that he wanted to do illustrations for a collector's edition. Céline liked the idea very much. So I arranged a meeting between them at Falstaff's in Montparnasse. Céline, Elisabeth Craig, and I, waited for Kokoschka, but in vain. Capricious, hard to pin down, you know what he was like. O. K. had obviously forgotten about the meeting. Too bad. The combination of Kokoschka-Céline might have produced something really stunning . . .

★   ★   ★

A letter Miller wrote to Roger Klein in September or October of 1934 sheds new light on the relationship between Céline and Miller. To my immense surprise, it contained a copy of a letter Céline had written to Henry about *Tropic*, the existence of which Frank Dobo was doubtless unaware:

Dear Roger,

I sent my book to Céline with a letter and immediately got a note back from him telling me that he would read my book with great interest, and that a quick glance had already intrigued him, etc. And then he said something that I didn't quite understand. I'll quote it for you, and if you understand its significance, let me know immediately, because I am dying from curiosity. I cite the letter in its entirety:

To my colleague:

I will be very happy to read your *Tropic*. Already what I have gotten through intrigues me and makes me want to read it all. Permit me to give you a small piece of advice about something I know fairly well. MAINTAIN A HEALTHY DISCRETION! MORE DISCRETION ALWAYS! Learn to be wrong — the world is filled with people who are right — and that is why it disheartens so.

Best Wishes,

L.-F. Céline

It's the underlined phrases that I don't understand [Miller had underlined the sentences Céline put in capital letters, and put a question mark after "disheartens" — *Au*]. The last word means, I suppose, a broken heart. But what did he mean by "your discretion?" Is he reproaching me for something?

In haste,

Henry

I do not know what interpretation, if any, Roger offered Miller regarding Céline's mysterious note. Céline was by nature more discreet than Miller, and one wonders if he was shocked by Miller's vaunted supervirility. The "discretion" that he counsels, might it have had something to do with that? The part of the letter to highlight, in my opinion, because it is even more cryptic, is *"Learn to be wrong — the world is filled with people who are right — and that is why it disheartens so."* Such a revealing phrase. "Learn to be wrong" was advice Céline followed his whole life, and contained within it lies his whole tragic fate. Indeed, Louis-Ferdinand never stopped repeating *"Learn to be wrong! Be Wrong!"* The critic Pascal Pia argued that Céline possessed the gift of putting oneself spontaneously in the wrong to a supreme degree, "thereby provoking the very hatred he knew he would become a victim to." At the age of twenty-five, Céline married the daugher of a director of the Ecole de Médecine. A brilliant career seemed to lie before him: a lucrative practice in a nice neighborhood, wealthy clientele, connections, fortune. But he shattered all that by taking off to Geneva, then Liverpool; at various points he turned up in the Cameroon, the United States, Canada, and Cuba. "Even more," he has Bardamu say in *Journey*, "I love to run after I don't know what, from drunken pride no doubt." Escape, escape forever! The obsession to pull up stakes the very second they get put down. So it was for *Journey to the End of Night.* Success, status, and money all came his way. But as soon as the left-wing parties and the Soviets began to celebrate him as the great revolutionary writer, the scourge of the bourgeoisie, the spiritual heir to Zola, he dismissed them with one violent swipe. *"Learn to be wrong!"* Upon his return from a visit to Moscow, he had only caustic remarks to offer about Soviet Russia. Scandalized, the Clichy town council, nearly

Henry Miller (1932)

Alfred Perlès (1932)

Hans Reichel

Lawrence Durrell

Anaïs Nin (1932)

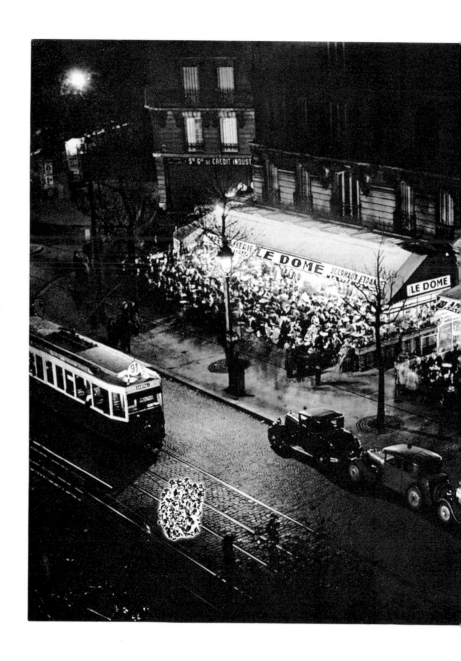

The Dôme and Boulevard Montparnasse (1932).

Girl at billiard table (1932).

Portrait of June given to me by Henry Miller (photographer unknown).

The beginning of the thirties.

Hôtel de la Montagne Sainte-Geneviève

Chez Suzy

"The Cemetery Montmartre, for example, shot from the bridge at night is a phantasmagoric creation of death flowering in electricity; the intense patches of night lie upon the tombs and crosses in a crazy patchwork of steel girders which fade with the sunlight into bright green lawns and flower beds and graveled walks. — From "The Eye of Paris""

"I think of chair because among all the objects which Brassaï has photographed his chair with the wire legs stands out with a majesty that is singular and disquieting. It is a chair of the lowest denomination, a chair which has been sat on by beggars and by royalty, by little trot-about whores and by queenly opera divas. It is a chair which the municipality rents daily to any and every one who wishes to pay fifty centimes for sitting down in the open air. A chair with little holes in the seat and wire legs which come to a loop at the bottom. The most unostentatious, the most inexpensive, the most ridiculous chair, if a chair can be ridiculous, which could be devised. Brassaï chose precisely this insignificant chair and, snapping it where he found it, unearthed what there was in it of dignity and veracity. THIS IS A CHAIR. Nothing more.   — From "The Eye of Paris"

Le Repos de la Montagne, located in Ménilmontant
(the photo was taken in the company of Léon-Paul Fargue in 1932).

Henry Miller, as he appeared at the door to my hotel room one day in 1932.

Brassaï in his laboratory (1932).

all of whose members were communists, forced him out of his clinic there. No matter! This volcano spews out its lava and slag on the left as freely as on the right, and it doesn't matter which! Finally, with *Bagatelles for a Massacre,* he succeeds in alienating everyone. His last friends and his most enduring supporters turn their backs on him. "*Learn to be wrong!*" Magnificent advice on how to create a void around oneself. The rest of Céline's story is well known. He died forgotten, outlawed, banished, despised. And this is exactly as he foresaw: "I will die in shame, ignominy, and poverty." By giving to his "colleague" the perfidious and Mephistophelian advice to "learn to be wrong," he was trying to condemn Miller to the same tragic fate he had predicted for himself.

The author of *Journey* was not indifferent to Henry: "I don't renounce Sartre," said Céline one day, "or Camus, or Miller — for all the good that has done me." He would also write that "poor Cendrars has been trying for the thirty years that I've known him to write a novel. He'll never do it — and neither will Miller." As for Henry, so great was his admiration for Céline that he placed him alongside another doctor — Rabelais. Both expressed their vision of the world with the same earthy honesty. Céline had the stature of Rabelais, thought Miller, but a Rabelais swept away on a river of invective that turns laughter into sarcasm, into screaming, raging, filthy curses — all products of a pen dipped in toilet bowls and vitriol.

During the two years of reprieve, Miller doubtless had time to think over Céline's advice. By degrees, *Tropic* turned into a pamphlet, a manifesto, or, as Miller defines it in the book itself, "a prolonged insult, a gob of spit in the face of Art, a kick in the pants to God, Man, Destiny, Time, Love, Beauty . . . what you will." Miller's impact on literature was initially far less shattering than Céline's — the first English edition of *Tropic* was published in near secrecy — but over time that impact grew to match it. The nearly simultaneous appearance of these two novels announced that change had come. Man's revolt against society, against those who would use him as they saw fit and sacrifice him to further their interests, was no longer latent; now it was open rebellion. In both Céline's incurable despair and Miller's unshakable optimism could be heard the same cry for help from a humanity being crushed by civilization, being ripped apart in the gears of what was called progress, humanity seeking desperately to reconnect its severed connections to the cosmos. Céline and Miller were the great agitators, and showed us the profound effect the "time of the assassins" was having on the human soul. *Journey to the End of Night* was Céline's great work, and *Tropic of Cancer* was Miller's. They had all the power, all the spontaneousness, of an explosive burst — of an emergence.

★   ★   ★

I ran into Henry several days after his novel had been published, and he looked radiant. He told me that everyone was calling *Tropic of Cancer* his first book, but that actually it was his fifth — it followed *The Twelve Eccentric Messengers* and three novels. He also told me that he had only brought a manuscript of one of the novels with him to Paris, and that a French publisher had misplaced it. It was, he said, his only copy. He saw symbolism in the loss.

I remember that in his room at Clichy, pinned to the wall, was this sentence from René Crevel: *Aucun risque n'est fatal!* ["No risk is fatal!"]. There is no doubt he took heart from it. He did indeed survive the "risk" of *Tropic*. Crevel, on the other hand, didn't survive his risks; the young surrealist poet committed suicide.

MILLER: The publication of my book is tremendously important to me. It's my *Season in Hell*. I hope it means an end to the long string of frustrations and humiliations. It's my last word on the subject of despair and revolt, I hope. A remedy for me that might also cure some of my readers. At least I hope so. I hope.

ME: How are sales?

MILLER: I went by Brentano's yesterday, on the Avenue de l'Opéra. Seeing your book displayed in the window gives you a strange sensation. Anyway, inside, a few readers had their noses between some of the uncut pages and were blushing from ear to ear. They're selling two or three copies a day. Not too bad, huh?

ME: Why *Cancer*?

MILLER: I spent two sleepless nights searching for a title to the thing. The word *cancer* has always obsessed me. Did you know, my dear Halasz, that in astrology and in Chinese symbolism the sign of cancer is tremendously important? Canker, cancer — both mean "crab." And the crab is the only creature to move sideways, to have the ability to move in every direction, even backwards. That has always fascinated me. [I, of course, was thinking about everything that Miller had told me about his desire to go backwards, to regress.] I believe that was why this zodiac sign was assigned to the poet by Chinese sages. But the cancer is also a symbol of the slow decomposition of civilization — as well as being its most representative disease. Three members of my family died of cancer.

★   ★   ★

When Henry moved into the Villa Seurat, he thought that it was a new beginning for him, that the "seismic shocks" of his life would now diminish in severity. This proved to be the case for the needs of the flesh and the belly, but certainly not for the spirit. The armada of "vultures" was only a memory of quieter days (or noisier ones) in Clichy. Compared to the Wepler, Boulevard Rochechouart, La Fourche, and the grand marketplace of sex that was Montmartre, Miller's new abode on the Left Bank was an oasis of calm and serenity. And even Montrouge Square (now Victor Basch Square), where Miller began spending his evenings in the company of a few friends, lacked the *belles de nuit* of his former haunts. At the Zeyer and sometimes at the Bouquet d'Alésia, where, before going home, Henry would down one last *demi*, the talk was much more about astrology, Asian thought, occult science, yoga, and Zen, than about sex and erotic women. This was the period when Miller found David Edgar, an experienced occultist who would initiate him into the arcane world of Asian philosophy.

Even though his book did not immediately bring him fame and fortune, Miller was happy. The recognition it brought him from a small circle of people consoled him — there was a flattering letter from T. S. Eliot, that note from Céline, fan mail from unknown admirers, and, two months after *Tropic* was published, Blaise Cendrars's "Unto Us an American Writer Is Born" appeared. "A royal book, an atrocious book, exactly the kind of book that I love best," wrote the poet of the *Man Struck By Lightning*. Rather than a review, what Cendrars offered Miller was more in the way of a "fraternal salute from one writer to another." "Even though written in English, and though the author is one hundred percent American," wrote Cendrars, "this book, because of the way it exposes people and things and speaks of them with gritty honesty . . . is profoundly French, and Henry

Miller is one of us in his spirit, in his writing, in the power of his gift, a writer as universal as any who have found ways of expressing in a book their private vision of Paris." Several weeks earlier, Miller had met Marcel Duchamp at an exhibition, and Duchamp had asked him if he might be interested in writing an article for a literary review. Henry had said no. It seems very possible that as a result of Miller's refusal, Duchamp had asked Cendrars to write his "salute" instead.

Sales of *Tropic of Cancer* were disappointing. Between September 1934 and July 1935, 1,300 copies of the book were sold. Still, Miller wasn't discouraged. The poor sales inspired him to come up with a few crazy publicity ideas — such as buying a mimeograph machine so that he could publish a pamphlet called "Henry Miller," containing every word that anyone had written or said about his book — letters, reviews, and so forth. The idea was to send the pamphlet at no charge to publishers, magazine editors, and critics around the world. The Miller that I knew at this period was electric with energy, strung as tight as a drum. Unrepentant and optimistic, he believed more than ever that he would become a celebrated writer. Events were urging him on and holding him back at the same time; he didn't know whether he was coming or going. He couldn't slow down, he would tell me. His head was bursting with ideas, and he was doing too much and was half dead on his feet. He would complain about terrible headaches, and say that his teeth were decalcifying because even at Villa Seurat there would be forty-eight-hour stretches when he wouldn't eat so much as a crust of bread. His only "metaphysical agony" being the possibility that he might die of starvation, Anaïs stuffed him with enough food so that he'd survive for at least another week, but she was often away traveling, or lost in her dreams, and sometimes forgot about her charge. Henry worked on half a dozen books at once, such as writing a new essay for *Max and the White Phagocytes* or new stories intended for *Tropic of Capricorn*, on which he had already begun work in Clichy. It was at Villa Seurat that he finished, and published in June 1936, *Black Spring*, which he dedicated to Anaïs. Miller thought the book revealed more about him than anything else he had ever written, and had even wanted to title it *Self Portrait*. He'd given part of the manuscript to Frank Dobo in 1933, accompanied by a note that read, "The black spring is the core of the whole book, which is the bitterest and wildest thing, and the most joyful and beautiful, that I have ever written. It's short and prophetic, and around thirty pages." For an epigraph he chose these words from Miguel de Unamuno: "Can I be as I believe myself or as others believe me to be? Here is where these lines become a confession in the presence of my unknown and unknowable me, unknown and unknowable for myself. Here is where I create the legend wherein I must bury myself." Miller would also attempt to bring out of the quagmire an unbelievable mass of notes for a book that he wanted to write on D. H. Lawrence. The first years at Villa Seurat were the most fertile of his life, and indeed he was to call them the "years of illumination."

★   ★   ★

While living in Clichy, Henry began the habit of writing down his literary projects on giant sheets of wrapping paper taped to the wall: outlines of books, with their principal characters; titles of works that he wanted to write; names of characters; cities he wanted to learn more about, countries he wanted to visit; publishers; magazines to look at; streets, areas yet to be discovered. On these same sheets he would write out, in big letters, every phrase and aphorism that had struck him, so that he could get used to the way they looked, and also new words he thought exotic to him, so that he could incorporate them into his vocabulary.

One day when I was looking at these enigmatic diagrams, he told me how much he needed these wall murals at eye level in order to see graphically, and in a certain order, the enormous mass of material he had in his head or in his notebooks. I particularly remember his graphic "map" for *Lawrence's Universe:* a hopeless tangle of notes, numbers, arrows, references that looked something like a medieval town with its winding streets. Henry had also written out, in chalk, the astrological chart Conrad Moricand drew up for him. His watercolors were also pinned up there. (The urge to paint had hounded him since childhood, but it took until 1929, the year before he left for Europe, to produce results.) June had gotten him George Grosz's *Ecce Homo,* and the book had made a profound impression upon him. He loved Turner's paintings, in which the colors of ocean and sky run together. His first teacher had been Emil Schnellock, his best friend while he was growing up and an artist and painter (Schnellock would be "Ulric" in his stories) who encouraged, guided, and inspired him. After Schnellock came Hans Reichel, who would initiate him in the finer points of watercolor. His last teacher was his friend Abe Rattner, his travel companion during a trip across the United States in 1940 (recounted in *The Air-Conditioned Nightmare*).

★　　★　　★

Each time I went to see Miller at Villa Seurat, I could already hear from the stairwell the hammering of his typewriter, which he struck at with frenzied fury. You almost wondered if it was the sound of his Underwood that carried the flow of his thoughts, the way a military march can carry a crowd. Any of his friends who surprised Henry writing away, in flagrante delicto, came away with the impression of a "writing machine" (as he calls himself in *Tropic of Cancer*) going at full tilt. Roger Klein once told me: "It ratatatated away like a machine gun. He was like a secretary practicing scales at a speed-typing competition. And the papers that spewed out one after the other! Did you ever look closely at them? Not one erasure or type-over! His works gushed out, as if a tap had been hooked up right to the source. What would Henry's writing have been like, I wonder, if it had been written out deliberately by hand rather than erupting out of his typewriter?"

A reasonable question, because although Henry wrote nearly all of his letters by hand, he could only write his manuscripts using a typewriter. Without it he was paralyzed. When he was teaching in Dijon, he begged Anaïs to send him a typewriter with an American keyboard as soon as she could. Otherwise, he wrote, his whole stay there would be fruitless. This fierce devotion to the typewriter can doubtless be explained by the speed with which he could transmit his thoughts, and by the immediate detachment of the text. Typewritten, it was not an extension of his body in the way something written by hand would be.

Paradoxically, if Miller was incapable of putting his thoughts on paper without his keyboard, those thoughts would only force themselves upon him when he was far from the machine. He spent hours sitting in front of his typewriter, waiting in vain for some inspiration. All he had to do was leave it and he'd be taken up in a whirlwind of ideas. Therein lies the drama of Henry Miller's writing life: not to be able to think except when he was walking around, and not to be able to nail down his thoughts except when he had his fingers on the keyboard. He lived constantly with the fear that he would lose his best ideas, and dreamed of being rich enough one day to afford to have a secretary follow him around when he walked and take dictation.

Though spontaneity took precedence over any concern about form, it would be a mistake to think that Miller didn't revise. He went back over his imaginative leaps with careful deliberation and reworked the imperfections. Afterward, he would retype the marked pages, as this gave him a final opportunity to make even more changes. He sometimes spent an entire day reworking one page.

★   ★   ★

As we've seen, the minute Henry landed someplace, he set out to explore his new turf. He already knew the 13th and 14th arrondissements, and began extending his morning rambles all the way to Paris's southern suburbs: Montrouge, Gentilly, Kremlin-Bicêtre, Ivry. One day, not far from Boulevard Kellermann, he happened on a small square called Place de Rungis. It was a strange, almost unreal place. The ironwork and the metal steps to a train depot looked as if they were planted there, creating a dreamlike setting. The streets around the square had strange names. For some months this "little square" took on the same aura for Henry that the "little phrase" did for Swann, and the "little section of wall" for Bergotte. "I always steered instinctively for the Place de Rungis," he wrote in *A Devil in Paradise*, "which in some mysterious way connected itself with certain phases of the film *L'Age d'Or*, and more particularly with Luis Buñuel himself." Alas, poor Place de Rungis! Destroyed, as were so many others like it, by the invasion of huge blocks of reinforced cement. The *bistrot-tabac* with its beautifully etched windows, the only ones of their kind, faithful reminders of the little square's original turn-of-the-century decor, has disappeared. (Happily, I was able to photograph them in time).

When he got home to his studio, his brain heated up, a cigarette burning his lips, Miller went straight for the keyboard — without even taking off his coat or scarf — turned on the faucet of his thoughts, and began to tap, tap, tap.

XI

Truth and Storytelling

When I read *Tropic of Cancer,* nearly all of whose actors and settings are familiar to me, I feel as if I'm entering the laboratory of Henry Miller's mind, the place in which real events and real people were reborn in his dense, muggy, subtropical prose. I myself appear on three of its pages, beginning with the lines, "Then one day I fell in with a photographer . . ."[1]

If I bring up myself at this point, it is only because doing so provides a direct view into the way storytelling works in Miller.

> Then one day I fell in with a photographer; he was making a collection of the slimy joints of Paris for some degenerate in Munich. He wanted to know if I would pose for him with my pants down, and in other ways. I thought of those skinny little runts, who look like

---

[1] At first, "The Eye of Paris" was the first part of *Tropic.* In this "trash can," as he liked to call his novel, Miller dumped in texts whose origins were very different, only to eliminate them later on. — *Au.*

bellhops and messenger boys, that one sees on pornographic post cards in little bookshop windows occasionally, the mysterious phantoms who inhabit the Rue
de la Lune and other malodorous quarters of the city. I
didn't like very much the idea of advertising my physiog
in the company of these élite. But, since I was assured
that the photographs were for a strictly private collection,
and since it was destined for Munich, I gave my consent.
When you're not in your home town you can permit
yourself little liberties, particularly for such a worthy mo-
tive as earning your daily bread. After all, I hadn't been so
squeamish, come to think of it, even in New York. There
were nights when I was so damned desperate, back there,
that I had to go out right in my own neighborhood and
panhandle.

We didn't go to the show places familiar to the tourists, but to the little joints where the atmosphere was
more congenial, where we could play a game of cards in
the afternoon before getting down to work. He was a good
companion, the photographer. He knew the city inside
out, the walls particularly; he talked to me about Goethe
often, and the days of the Hohenstaufen, and the massacre of the Jews during the reign of the Black Death.
Interesting subjects, and always related in some obscure
way to the things he was doing. He had ideas for scenarios
too, astounding ideas, but nobody had the courage to
execute them. The sight of a horse, split open like a
saloon door, would inspire him to talk of Dante or
Leonardo da Vinci or Rembrandt; from the slaughterhouse at Villette he would jump into a cab and rush me to
the Trocadéro Museum, in order to point out a skull or a
mummy that had fascinated him. We explored the 5th,
the 13th, the 19th and the 20th *arrondissements* thoroughly. Our favorite resting places were lugubrious little
spots such as the Place Nationale, Place des Peupliers,
Place de la Contrescarpe, Place Paul-Verlaine. Many of

these places were already familiar to me, but all of them I now saw in a different light owing to the rare flavor of his conversation. If today I should happen to stroll down the Rue du Château-des-Rentiers, for example, inhaling the fetid stench of the hospital beds with which the 13th *arrondissement* reeks, my nostrils would undoubtedly expand with pleasure, because, compounded with that odor of stale piss and formaldehyde, there would be the odors of our imaginative voyages through the charnel house of Europe which the Black Death had created.

It is true that I went on several nocturnal walks with Henry, but the only time we planned to spend an evening together in what he terms the "malodorous quarters" hadn't worked out. Never once did I go to a bordello with Henry; and never did I use him as a model for any pornographic pictures. For one thing, I did not do pornography; I was doing a photographic study of human behavior, and that was why I frequented the centers of pleasure and vice that had so captured Miller's imagination.

It was therefore from my photographs that he imagined we had gone to those "slimy joints" together, not because we had actually done so. Nor was I acquainted with "Miss Hamilton's joint" on that little street behind Notre-Dame-de-Lorette, where in the novel he takes the rich Hindu, or with the "little 20-sou place" in Aubervilliers. Among the bordellos that Henry describes in his work, I knew only the ones on the Rue Sainte-Apolline, near the Porte Saint-Denis, and the Sphinx, in Montparnasse. But, again, we never went to these places together. And that afternoon game of cards we played "before getting down to work" — he saw it in one of the photographs I took at the Suzy, on Rue Grégoire-de-Tours, in the Saint-Germain-des-Prés section of town.

He was a good companion, the photographer. He knew the city inside out, the walls particularly. This is true. At the time, Paris had few secrets from me. I knew every inch of it, having explored it *quartier* by *quartier*, especially at night. "The walls particularly" is a reference to the photographs of graffiti I had started putting together in 1930, and that I published with my book, titled *Du mur des cavernes aux murs d'usine* [*From Cave Walls to Factory Walls*], a title suggested to me by Paul Eluard in the literary magazine *Minotaure*, in 1934. In "The Eye of Paris" Miller wrote, "He explores with equal patience, equal interest, a crack in the wall or the panorama of a city."

He talked to me about Goethe often . . . Very true. Goethe's work is one of my anchors, and I often told Miller of my admiration for it. No easy task. Henry was then in his nihilist phase, and felt that all the classics — Shakespeare, Homer, Goethe — should be heaped into the same bucket. "Did you know," I would tell him, "that when German nationalism was on the rise against Napoleon and France, Goethe was perhaps the only German writer who refused to give in to it? He was the only one not to be taken up in the collective hysteria that was carrying everyone else away. The only one to oppose the way 'love of country' — already a sacred phrase — had degenerated into passion. He later told Eckermann how impossible it would have been for him to hate the country to whose art and culture he owed so much. Raising himself above nations and their conflicts, Goethe courageously believed and proclaimed that national hate reduces people to the lowest order of humanity. So you see Henry," I would conclude, "his was a kindred spirit to yours."

"I know what we're supposed to owe to Goethe," Miller would retort, "and I know I should admire him for it. But I just can't bring myself to do it and don't think I ever will.

That Goethe approached the ideal of the free spirit, that he was a 'man' — the highest praise Napoleon could bestow — all this I happily acknowledge, but unfortunately for him and me, he was also too much of a super-bourgeois, a respectable citizen, a valet to princes, and you must admit that he was well known to be an insufferable pedant and a bore. So he's not my type. I oppose his placid, serene, and Olympian attitude, and I think I'm right to do so. Myself, I prefer Rabelais or Swift or Cervantes, or poets such as Wordsworth, Tennyson, and above all Walt Whitman."

"You're always harping on the stuffed-shirt, Olympian attitude of the older Goethe," I would reply, "but it was a mask, a mask he used to protect himself against that army of bores who were all over Weimar. If he'd been any less offputting, they would have eaten him alive. Actually, Goethe was happiest in the company of simple people, unpretentious people, the uncorrupted. He enjoyed their way of doing things, and their warmth. And do you think he loved only high-society women? With the exception of Madame von Stein — who was a friend rather than a lover — he thought they were beneath him. Anyone who was snobbish, priggish, and starchy, he avoided like the plague. And even in Weimar, this man who was a minister and a friend of the prince, a man who could have married a princess, had he so desired — to the indignation of society, of course — ended up living with a young girl of no means, a flower girl from a poor family. Goethe was in love with Christiane and wanted to live with her. He couldn't have given a tinker's damn about what people would say. Wasn't this a sign of courage, even heroism, given his times? To shack up with someone like that, in a city like Weimar? And who do you think took the most offense at this, who shouted scandal loudest? It wasn't the court sycophants, or the bigots, or the nitpickers. It was Schiller! That's right — Schiller the 'revolutionary,' the 'emancipated man,' the 'flag waver of liberty,' the 'bene-factor to man,' which were the titles the Assemblée had conferred upon him. What do you think about that? Reading the correspondence between Goethe and Schiller, I was stunned to discover that the author of *Brigands* categorically refused to acknowledge Goethe's mistress, whom he treated like a leper. Not so much as a 'best wishes' to his 'concu-bine'! Goethe never failed to convey his best wishes to Charlotte, Schiller's wife, and in every single one of his letters. Not one word of concern when Christiane was giving birth to a baby — she had five of them — not a word of sympathy when Goethe lost four of them, one right after the other — bah! They were just bastards, right? — or any ac-knowledgment of the grief his friend must have felt. Goethe was the one who was the emancipated man, the freethinker, and Schiller the bigot, the snob, the 'valet to princes.' "

In Miller's eyes, Goethe had committed the fundamen-tal sin of being draped in the shroud of two centuries' worth of veneration. The "classics" had had their day and had nothing left to teach us. In fact, they were harmful, mind-destroying, poisonous. Best to destroy every one of their books. He even criticized the *Iliad* for having so much car-nage in it. No, thought Miller, we're wasting our time think-ing about these has-beens, and we have to protect ourselves from the tyrannical authority they still exert over us. The only figure to survive his general massacre of the ancients was Rabelais, whom he adored for his deep laughter, his humor, his love of banquets and women, and especially for his rich and unbridled freedom of expression. Miller also spared Petronius because of the audacity and license of his *Satyricon*.

When Miller had gotten through his nihilistic period, his view of Goethe became much more conciliatory. He even admitted that unconsciously Goethe had been his greatest example. One day he confessed that when he had read *Wilhelm Meister,* he had been profoundly moved by the novel's autobiographical element. What Goethe was trying to do was rediscover "life's traces." He'd never forgotten that phrase. Deep down, that was what he also was trying to do. Like Goethe, he was a "searcher for truth."

I am not in the least trying to suggest that I alone deserve all the credit for turning Miller around on the subject of Goethe. Perlès and young Renaud in Dijon both struggled to convert him. In the end, convert him we did, and his glowing praise of Goethe in the following passage from *Hamlet* reveals the extent to which we succeeded:

> Nothing is more certain and unshakable, more solid and convincing, than the living words of the man Goethe. Whatever failed to come off, to make itself understood, as it were, never impairs the original spirit. Goethe lives and in him the truth, Goethe's truth, which I understand and accept. Goethe lives in me, not through understanding, but through a magic contagion which the power and sincerity of the man conveyed through language . . . But Goethe never doubted himself, nor the efficacy and the value of his words. He had the courage to put down what he himself did not understand, knowing that he was drawing from a divine source which could not fail eventually to make manifest its meaning. This I admire in the good Goethe. What is dark and oracular here bespeaks something beyond the self. The great spirit of the man breaks through the body to ally itself with Nature.

Later, Miller also wrote a letter of apology about Goethe, but the letter, which he had sent to Fred, was destroyed in the bombing of London. All that remains is this early elegy from *Aller-Retour New York*:

We will stand on the last stanza of Faust and get that ever-higher feeling. Towards the eternal feminine, which, after all, is only the drag and pull of Nature, which, when one becomes altogether Godlike, says: Be yourself! Touch the earth! Let us, therefore, rise in song and fall with the parachute. Goethe, standing on that last stanza, commanded a greater vista than any aviator has yet commanded. He was standing on the higher middle ground, the metaphysical tableland which is between heaven and earth. Poised on the eternal moment, calm, sure, prince of men, he surveyed past and future. He saw the spiral motion which obtains in all realms, commencing with the astral and finishing with the astral. He saw it in its unendingness. Goethe was an aviator a hundred years before his time. He learned to stand still — *and sing.*

Let us return to *Tropic of Cancer: [H]e talked to me about Goethe often, and the days of the Hohenstaufen, and the massacre of the Jews during the reign of the Black Death. Interesting subjects, and always related in some obscure way to the things he was doing.* We actually never did talk about these subjects, Henry and I, though suddenly I realize I may know why he was thinking about the Black Death. When he was writing *Tropic of Cancer,* the plague was a very fashionable topic. It particularly fascinated the psychoanalyst René Allendy and the actor Antonin Artaud; the latter had asked Anaïs to find the "Plague Chronicles" for him in the Bibliothèque Nationale, because he was to give a lecture on it at the Sorbonne. What fascinated them was not so much the plague itself — though its victims had numbered 25 million in Europe — but its effects: to those terrorized by death, life seemed precious and sweet. People let themselves go. They tried to outdo one another in creating works of art. For Allendy and Artaud, the Black Plague might have been the most desirable thing to have happened to society; its power of dissolution fascinated them even more. Plagues changed society more radically than any revolution ever did. Violence and vice took on unbelievable dimensions during this time of horror, in which, according to Petrarch, there were "more dead than there were living to bury them."

Artaud gave his lecture, "The Theater and the Plague," at the Sorbonne on April 6, 1933. I went to it with Miller and Anaïs.

"Once the plague had settled itself in the city," Artaud said, "normal boundaries began to break down. There was no more garbage collection, no army, no police, no municipality. Bonfires were lit to burn the dead whenever there were enough free hands to do it." The audience was impressed by the energy and enthusiasm with which Artaud described a city under the plague: decaying cadavers, the stench of putrescence, the delirium of those who were suffering, the frantic sex, the superstitious practices, the ceaseless parade of flagellators, the massacre of Jews. No part that Artaud ever played was closer to his heart than the one he performed during that lecture. Near the end, right there on the podium, he began to imitate a plague sufferer writhing in agony. His face muscles convulsed, his eyes bulged, his arms and legs stiffened. Foaming at the mouth, he screamed and ranted like a man possessed. And that was the origin of the Black Death about which I never spoke with Miller.

He had ideas for scenarios too, astounding ideas, but nobody had the courage to execute them. The sight of a horse, split open like a saloon door, would inspire him to talk of Dante or Leonardo da Vinci or Rembrandt; from the slaughterhouse at Villette he would jump into a cab and rush me to the Trocadéro Museum, in order to point out a skull or a mummy that had fascinated him. Nothing in this passage is true, with the exception of the "astounding ideas" for scenarios. Perhaps Miller wanted to show that I was fascinated by many things, and in no particular order, and by the connections I tried to find between them. The idea that I would have to specialize in any one particular thing horrified me.

Here, at any rate, is one of the scenarios I had come up with: Imagine that the earth has grown dark and a new ice age has descended. The only survivors are two tribes of Eskimos, natural enemies and at war with each other, both of which flee the torments of the Arctic regions for more temperate climates. They end up in the country of the *roi de Soleil.* Their most sacred object — handed down from one generation to the next and given by the dying chief to his firstborn son — is a miniature replica of the Eiffel Tower, the kind tourists buy. Some time after their flight south, the sun having reappeared, the two tribes make camp in the snow. While breaking the surface of the ice with a tool, in order to make an igloo, the young chief of the first tribe strikes something metallic. The top of the Eiffel Tower. He keeps his discovery a secret, and every night he goes out and digs deeper and deeper, until one night he finds a staircase leading him down into a gigantic ice cave that has formed over an immense city. The city is deserted but preserved intact. He shows it to the others. Someone accidentally hits a switch at a power station, and suddenly the dead city lights up. The Eskimos move into Paris and continue with their life — our life — but without knowing any of our habits or the significance of even the most everyday objects, such as a telephone, a corkscrew, a dish rack, a car, a plane. Everything is strange to them.

The scenario would make a futuristic film, perhaps, but one that moves backward, in a sense. It is about our life being lived by people who lack the key to it. Their ignorance of everything so familiar and dear to us would give it, so I thought, comic overtones, even poignant ones. One scene among others: When the city's new inhabitants discover the Louvre, they rip apart paintings by Rubens,

Da Vinci, Rembrandt, Vélasquez in order to make tents out of the canvases. Another scene: A battle between the two tribes erupts in the Grévin Museum over a wax figure of Maurice Chevalier sporting his boater, whom they have identified as the Sun King himself; a scene of drunkenness and orgy at the Museum of Natural History among the stuffed animals and skeletons. Everyone has gotten drunk from drinking the formaldehyde in the sealed jars containing snakes, lizards, and fetuses. That was one of my "stunning ideas" Miller was recalling.[2]

We explored the 5th, the 13th, the 19th and the 20th arrondissements thoroughly. Our favorite resting places were lugubrious little spots such as the Place Nationale, Place des Peupliers, Place de la Contrescarpe, Place Paul-Verlaine. Many of these places were already familiar to me, but all of them I now saw in a different light owing to the rare flavor of his conversation. If today I should happen to stroll down the Rue du Château-des-Rentiers, for example, inhaling the fetid stench of the hospital beds with which the 13th arrondissement reeks, my nostrils would undoubtedly expand with pleasure, because, compounded with that odor of stale piss and formaldehyde, there would be the odors of our imaginative voyages through the charnel house of Europe which the Black Death had created.

Of this entire passage I can corroborate only our shared passion for the malodorous parts of town, for the "little dark corners" and their "sinister beauty," to borrow the phrase from Jacques Prévert. Miller returns to the thought in the following passage from his introduction to my book *Histoire de Marie*: "After my nightly rambles in his company to the seamy parts of the capital, I returned home, as usual, in a sort of fever. Several hours spent with him and one had the

---

[2] Translator's note: In the original French edition, Brassaï recounts this "scenario" in a footnote rather than in the body of his text.

impression of being dragged into a great sieve, which would retain a little of everything that contributes to the exaltation of life."

But if Miller viewed certain parts of Paris "in a different light," I am convinced this was not because of the "rare flavor" of my conversation, but because of my photographs.

Another example of Miller's storytelling can be found in a letter he wrote to Durrell, in which he talks about our friend Louis Tihanyi, the man who had introduced us:

> [O]ne morning, just as I've struck the right rhythm, who walks in on me but Tihanyi, the deaf painter, remember? He tells me in his cluck-cluck language (which he always supposed we understood, but no one did, not even his Hungarian friends) that I should go right on writing, he would talk to me as I wrote. And by God, I did! And it was amazing that I wrote as well as I did — nothing lost, as I said before. He talked for twenty minutes while I polished off two or three pages — of "The Wild Park," I believe it was now. All he had come for was to tell me he had fixed a goulash for me.

It isn't quite fair to say that no one understood Tihanyi, "not even his Hungarian friends," for I understood him with perfect ease. So did Miller. Otherwise why did he write one sentence later that Tihanyi had told him to keep on writing and "by God, I did?" I am certain that this incident and the invitation were true. Tihanyi loved cooking and hated eating alone. He would very often go down to Montparnasse to look for a willing victim.

"When I got there that evening," Miller continues in the letter, "he was lying beside the telephone, dead." First of all, Tinhanyi couldn't have been lying beside the telephone because he didn't have a telephone. Second, he couldn't have been lying there dead because he died in

Cochin Hospital three days after having been taken there with meningitis.

Why would Miller need to twist the facts this way — and not even in a work of fiction, but in a letter to a friend? It seems hard to understand. However, this same letter to Durrell gives us a clue. He talks about death, which was something he rarely did: "All I was trying to say, bedazzled as I was, and it was like trying to put a knife into a crevice, was: 'What's it all about?' After the last line, *what*? After the television appearances, after the Academie, after the Nobel Prize, *what*?" In other words, it was while he had the void on his mind that Miller made up that story about Tihanyi talking about goulash in the morning and lying dead near his telephone that night. The novelist in Miller needed to fictionalize, to drive home his point to the reader — Lawrence Durrell, in this case — and to give urgency to that searing question, "What's it all about? After the last line, *what*?" Miller goes on to say that "looking back over my more tumultuous writings I began to wonder if perhaps I was not trying to hide something? Or perhaps I was hiding from myself. You know, for example, that when you are 'emotional' you're not really feeling. You're pumping it up. You put something outside that should be inside."

Another instance of dramatic distortion involves "The Eye of Paris." By the time he had begun his portrait of me, he had already transformed me in his mind. Why else would he have asked whether or not I wanted the character to have my name? He warned me that the portrait was going to be a little "wild," a bit "extravagant," and wanted to know if I preferred him to use some other name besides Brassaï. Henry was telling me not to be too picky about accuracy.

His portrait of me is indeed wild and extravagant. It is also flattering beyond all proportion. Yet, in "The Eye of Paris," I have to say that Miller has described my artistic vision with rare accuracy and total comprehension. I was very intrigued by a strange character Miller discusses in the essay, the character who was the reason for our meeting. He is called the "human cockroach."

> It happens that the man who introduced me to Brassai is a man who has no understanding of him at all, a sort of human cockroach living out his dream of the 18th century. He knows all the Metro stations by heart, can recite them backwards for you, line by line; he can give you the history of each *arrondissement*, can tell you precisely where and how one street intersects another, can give you the genesis of every statue and monument in Paris. But he has absolutely no feeling for the streets, no wanderlust, no curiosity, no reverence. He secretes himself in his room and lives out in imagination the hermeneutic life of the 18th century.
>
> I mention this only as an example of the strange fatality by which two men of kindred spirit are sometimes brought together. I mention it by way of showing that even the despised cockroach serves a purpose in life. I see that the cockroach living out its dream of the 18th century can serve as a link to bind the living.

Who is this "human cockroach"? Tihanyi? Perlès? Neither of them corresponds completely to the description. I have racked my brain trying to solve the puzzle. Knowing that I might be perplexed, Henry wrote me and said, "I have to tell you that the cockroach is not a character that you know, nor one you could imagine." But the question remains, why invent such a character? This is clearly another example of Miller fictionalizing the facts. In addition to a cockroach, there is a spider — me:

> In the very heart of it, like a spider luring me to its lair, there lived all the while this man Brassai whom I was

destined to meet. I remember vividly how, when I first came to Paris, I wandered one day to his hotel looking for a painter . . . I had to return to America, come back to France again, starve, roam the streets, listen to silly, idiotic theories of life and art, take up with this failure and that, and finally surrender to the cockroach before it was possible to know the man who like myself had taken in Paris without effort of will, the man who, without my knowing it, was silently slaving away at the illustrations for my books.

His need to create the cockroach, and that description of how he had been to my hotel before we had met (another story, I would guess) stemmed from his need to fictionalize our meeting, to attribute it to fate. The cockroach was invented as an agent of fate.

Such distortions abound in Miller's work. Yet another example: Miller often talked about the time he worked as a gravedigger in Queens. The truth is that he never dug graves to bury dead people. He dug holes for the Parks Department, so that they could plant trees. But a gravedigger is a far more romantic figure than a landscape gardener. It brings to mind Hamlet, standing over a freshly dug grave, holding the skull of Yorick and wondering, What's it all about? *What's it all about?*

XII

"Autobiography Is the Purest Romance"

At first, Miller's cavalier treatment of the truth troubled and shocked me, and I wasn't alone. Another was Hen Van Gelre, a Dutch writer who was one of Henry's most avid followers — and who has been publishing for some years the *International Henry Miller Letters*, a review devoted entirely to Miller. When he discovered that Miller had deliberately distorted the truth about him in one of his stories, he felt used and duped. In an article titled "The Language of Life," published in the journal *Synthèse*, he concluded that Henry was simply more enamored of story than of truth, and that one should simply not look for accuracy in his work. For Van Gelre, that conclusion brought with it some bitterness: "I have to admit that this was a particularly poignant discovery for me, a discovery that somewhat reduced the importance of Miller's work in my eyes." Since this "discovery," he wrote, he can no longer see in Miller the "purest incarnation of the writer of today."

Yet another was Anaïs. In the beginning she thought Miller the paragon of truth: "He speaks in the first person, uses the names of his friends, and rejects fiction and its laws." How bewildering it was to discover how much he distorted the truth. She was stupefied by the pages that he devoted to June in *Tropic of Capricorn*, the June that she had known herself: "It was no longer June but some character born in Henry's imagination." So, too, she could not figure out which version of the truth was contained in "Via Dieppe-Newhaven." Had Miller really been June's victim? At the very place where they were supposed to have had a bitter argument, Anaïs had seen them sitting together and drinking happily. "It threw me into deep perplexity," she wrote. "Which version of the story was a lie?" (*Diary*, vol. 2).

For his part, Miller always insisted that he sought the truth, that his narratives were true autobiography, and that his hero, the "I" of the stories, is always Henry Miller himself. He writes in *Hamlet*, "But when I do beg, borrow, steal, or prostitute myself, in order to earn a living, I don't set up an alter ego on which to shove the blame. I admit that it was I, Henry Miller, who did the lying, the thieving, the cajoling, the this or that, whatever it may be. I can look back upon my actions and deplore them, I can develop a certain amount of guilt about them, but I don't deny them." What could be clearer, more reassuring? Fiction, he said, horrified him, and so of course everyone expected sincerity and probity in his work, an absolute respect for the facts. When those who had imagined him the "apostle of the truth" discovered that the facts had been manipulated, they felt deceived and disappointed. By trying to pass lies off as truth and engaging in false advertising, wasn't Miller committing a terrible mistake?

Proust was cagier. The "Marcel" of the novel is never Proust himself, but a creation, a creation, as he would say over and over again, on whom should fall all responsibility and blame. Though his characters were inspired by real people, they were, he insisted, figures from his imagination. In fact, Proust's insistence that everything is invented in *Remembrance* was as hearty as Miller's insistence that his autobiographical narratives were based on truth. One can't help wondering if Miller wouldn't have been better off calling his stories *novels*, if this wouldn't have provided a way of avoiding unfortunate misunderstandings. How wise Goethe was not to title his autobiography *The Truth About My Life*, but instead *Poetry and Truth About My Life*, indicating right from the start the part that both fiction and invention would play. Louis Aragon called the story of his relationship with Matisse not *Henri Matisse*, but *Henri Matisse, A Novel*, making it sound almost like a literary hoax. The writer who writes his autobiography becomes the historian of his life. He is not supposed to make things up. He is supposed to stick scrupulously to what happened. Can a writer of Miller's stature be an objective, impartial historian of his life? Aragon thought not: "I am close to thinking of autobiographers as forgers," he wrote in *Théâtre/Roman*. "Honesty, without any doubt, would demand that most books being called memoirs be called novels, or, more accurately, novelistic." Curiously, Miller seems to have shared Aragon's opinion: "[N]o artist has ever succeeded in rendering nature on canvas, just as no author has ever truly been able to give us his life and thoughts," he noted in his essay "They Were Alive and They Spoke to Me." "Autobiography is the purest romance." "I began my writing career with the intention of telling the truth about myself," he writes in that essay on Rider Haggard. "What a fatuous task! What can possibly be more fictive than the story of one's life?" But if this is so, if a writer, truthful though he be, must of necessity distort certain events in his life, such as by making them more tumultuous or enimagtic or incomprehensible, why in heaven's name does Miller repeat ad nauseum that he's not writing novels but about what has "happened" to him in life. Is this not flagrant self-contradiction?

I think not. *Truth* and *reality* are not terms that can be defined in any conventional way in Miller's work. Reality is limitless and indefinable. It is never raw fact, which, Miller believed, was actually nothing but surface. Facts offer only their own version of events, and it would be a mistake to assume that human documents — intimate diaries, auto-biographical jottings — place us squarely in the heart of the matter. Reality must include thoughts, memories, dreams, everything that one can imagine or invent about a subject. "Fiction is always closer to reality than fact." Facts are feelings and thoughts — they are assimilated and digested. Life, therefore, cannot be grasped either by realism or by naturalism, but only through dreams, symbols, and storytelling. Because historical fact is not what happened, but what people's imaginations make of what has happened, reality is myth and legend. Hence the paradox of Miller's believing that works called "realistic" or "naturalistic" are really packs of lies, and that those in which the pure imagination consti-tutes the "real" (however we define it), such as in Rider Haggard's *She*, Balzac's *Séraphita*, and Alain-Fournier's *Le Grand Meaulnes* [*The Lost Domain*], offer a reality that is "richer, denser."

Miller never believed the truth to derive from a precise notation of facts and events, but instead from the flood of images that are unleashed in his imagination by these facts, from what he finds within, from what he wants to give of himself. He would agree with Aragon that "nothing is ever more lifelike than our imagination, our pure imagination." Or else, "We can only capture the truth through the power of the imagination." With this in mind we should approach

Miller's pronouncements, some of which are paradoxes worthy of Xenon of Eleus. One can lie and tell the truth, one can tell the truth and lie. To Anaïs, who admonished him for his myth-making, he writes, "So what?" His lies contain the truth of what he wants to say about himself.

There is therefore no contradiction, no incompatibility between truth and fiction, between what is authentic and what is imagined. The flight of the imagination begins at the very moment of perception. One could say of Miller what Gide said of Céline: "The reality that he depicts is the hallucination that reality provokes."

★　　★　　★

But while Miller makes a virtue of necessity, professing that reality is only a pretext for giving life to his obsessions and his hallucinations, and an excuse to make ample use of his storytelling gifts, he doesn't dwell on it. Sometimes he could even admit that his overactive imagination was a flaw, preventing him from seeing things as they really were, rather than purely as a reflection of his mind. So quickly does his art take over and cloud his vision of facts and events that when he looks at his notes later on, he no longer remembers what was really said and felt, and what was imagined. He could not control the moment; once his imagination seized the reins, his mind raced into the might-be, the could-be, the fantastic, the baroque, the unreal. It is, I believe, a common trait among great storytellers. It also might explain all of Balzac's failures with *real* life. The novelist Jean Giono was also suspected of using deceit in his stories about "real" people: "I force myself to stick as closely as possible to common everyday facts," he wrote in an article published in *Journal* in 1944. "My taste for making things up leads to an obscuring lyricism . . . Describe what happens, however banal. Express it quickly and in the most accurate way possible. Invent nothing. Submit yourself to the object." Trying not to hide behind the subjects and characters one is presenting; forgoing every thumbprint, every trace of the author; resisting all smugness, all embellishment; being but a witness to *what is*. All these represent the opposite pole from which Henry Miller, with what one might even call nostalgia, turned his back. Chance would have it that I be the one whom he thought embodied the expression "submit yourself to the subject." The true subject of "The Eye of Paris" is not me, but his nostalgia for what he is not. By drawing me, he is drawing himself — but *en négatif*.

The essay begins: "Brassaï has that rare gift which so many artists despise — *normal* vision. He has no need to distort or deform, no need to lie or to preach. He would not alter the living arrangement of the world by one iota; he sees the world precisely as it is and as few men in the world see it because seldom do we encounter a human being endowed with normal vision." There, in a nutshell, is the other extreme to Miller's vision, which, disdaining "normal" vision, needs to distort and to twist, to lie and to preach, and which captures the world not as it is, but as he imagines it to be. Another passage is even more explicit:

> The desire which Brassaï so strongly evinces, a desire *not* to tamper with the object but regard it as it is, was this not provoked by a profound humility, a respect and reverence for the object itself? The more the man detached from his view of life, from the objects and identities that make life, all intrusion of individual will and ego, the more readily and easily he entered into the multitudinous identities which ordinarily remain alien and closed to us. By depersonalizing himself, as it were, he was enabled to discover his personality everywhere in everything.

To praise "profound humility," "respect," "reverence for the object," a distance from all "intrusion of individual will and ego," "depersonalization" — all qualities that until then had been the objects of Miller's scorn and rebuke — was this not to draw his own portrait in *negative*? This whole passage is a paraphrase of a line from Goethe that particularly struck me, and that I adopted as my credo. I quote from memory: "The objects have slowly lifted me to their height." I must have quoted this to Henry at some point. Whatever else it does, the passage reveals clearly his perplexity and bewilderment at being faced with a vision of things so alien to his own.

It also expresses his doubts and perplexities:

> Perhaps this is not the method of art. Perhaps art demands the wholly personal, the catalytic power of will. *Perhaps*. All I know is that when I look at these photographs which seem to have been taken at random by a man loath to assert any values except what were inherent in the phenomena, I am impressed by their authority. I realize in looking at his photos that by looking at things aesthetically, just as much as by looking at things moralistically or pragmatically, we are destroying their value, their significance.

Miller's essay builds toward the apotheosis of the cosmological eye: "The cosmologic eye, persisting through wrack and doom, impervious, inchoate, *seeing only what is*." Miller himself underlined *seeing only what is*.

XIII

The "Voice"

Miller once told me that *Tropic of Capricorn, Plexus,* and especially *Nexus* were filled with odd bits and pieces that seemed to have found their way in without forethought or premeditation. These bits and pieces had their origins in the flood of memories that sometimes washed over him, particularly late at night. He had no choice but to get up, get a notebook, then spend hour after hour copying down the fully formed sentences that came pouring out. He was in a sort of a trance, innocent of what might be coming next. He always said that when he read those texts later on he was as flabbergasted and as shocked as any reader might be.

That was how Miller's most beautiful works came to life — in a rush, tumbling out of him like a "sack of coal." Creating meant tapping into a source and turning on a faucet, not agonizing about sentence structure. The process always took him by surprise — he was a transciber, a kind of Mohammed, an adherent to the dictates of an unseen force that had seized control of his hand. That was how he felt about his whole writing life. "It oozed out like milk from a coconut," says the narrator in *Plexus*. "I had nothing to do with it. Someone else was in charge. I was merely the receiving station transmitting it to the blue." At other moments he had the feeling, as he told Durrell in a letter, that "some panel inside one slid open, the musicians are there, the note is sounded, the walls give way, the images beckon — and you find yourself saying it without knowing it."

This unseen force, which sometimes he calls the Voice, sometimes the Dictate, sometimes the Other — making one think of Rimbaud's *I is an other* — would arrive in a fever of inspiration. His mind becomes inflamed. Soon there is a "flood," an "avalanche," a "hemorrhage," or a "fire" that cannot be put out. The ideas come galloping out with such speed that there is no way of corralling them. "It was as though a huge wheel inside me had begun to revolve," he wrote in *Plexus*. Often Miller could content himself with the thought that he had written something — even if he had only written it in his head. He believed that his dream-works were better than the ones he succeeded in getting down on paper. The latter were but "pale imitations."

In the calm after the visitation of the muses, Miller would reread what he'd written and find in it the trace of another hand. He was convinced that *we* create nothing, that writing happens only *through* us and *to* us. The same prodigious debauchery, the same profusion that can be found in nature, also exists in our own minds, which are a jungle of exuberant ideas. Henri Michaux also believes in the turbulence of ideas, and in the blinding speed with which they appear and then spin off, making their transcription impossible. One of the qualities of the Other is its suddenness, its unheralded arrival. It might overtake Miller while he was shaving, eating, talking, or relieving himself in the bathroom (indeed, the toilet seems to be one of the demon's favorite places). Most of the time, however, the Voice came to him when he was out walking, as it had for Rousseau and Nietzsche. The author of *Zarathustra* was unable to compose while sitting at a worktable; it was during his walks, during the rhythmic movement of the muscles, like a motor priming the body with a magnetizing fluid, that could make the sparks spring up to his brain. In *Ecce Homo*, Nietzsche sketched an outline for a science as yet in an embryonic state, which we might call the "physiology of thought." We recognize the beneficial influence that cleanliness has on certain minds — or coffee, tobacco, alcohol, drugs, or any of those *dérèglements* recommended by Rimbaud. Goethe was taken by surprise when Schiller told him that the smell of rotten apples provided him with a source of inspiration, a stimulant for thought.

Walking was Henry's stimulant; that was when the Voice would come, and since he was unable to focus his thoughts except on the typewriter, as we have seen, he was forced to rush back home. As soon as he got there he would pounce immediately on the keyboard in a "fusillade of all the fingers." It was always the same — in Paris, in New York, or in Big Sur. Emptying his mind became as compelling a need as emptying his bowels. Sometimes he had to jump into a cab, as happened once in Jacksonville, so strongly had the need to get down the "crazy, devilish" thoughts suddenly come upon him. They had been inspired by the ugliness of a public park he'd just been walking through.

★   ★   ★

Miller attributed many of the obscene parts of his stories to the Voice. He told me that they came to him when he was in a *secondary state*, caught up in an erotic dream. No writer, after all, can match the obscenity of a dream, no matter how hard he tries. Dreams don't enter through the front door. They slip in unnoticed and head straight for the satisfaction of desire. Wherever you are — at a dinner party, for example — without any warning whatsoever, a dream has us hiking up some young woman's dress and plunging our hand between her thighs. This imaginary feel wakes us up, our heart beating wildly, the sheets wet. (Can anyone solve the mystery of the wet dream, I wonder? A dream can mercilessly push even the shyest of men into the all-devouring world of sex. How can it do that — without the actual process and mechanics of "making love"?) Miller's "little bursts of obscenity," as he refers to them in a letter to Durrell, have to be put into the context of the dreamlike aura surrounding all his writing, which goes from one image to another, changing places, mixing past and present, confusing the living and the dead, moving from obscurity to sudden clarity, bringing murky events and characters into the light and portraying them with an acuity and realness we rarely see in our waking state. In *Sexus*, at one point, he dreams of Una Gifford, his long-lost love: "Her face had become like a heavy flower caught in darkness; it seemed transfixed by its own suffused glow ... The pallor of her skin was heightened by the marble glow that the smoldering embers of memory awakened. The head turned slowly on the almost indistinguishable stem. The lips were parted in thirst; they were extraordinarily vivid and vulnerable. It seemed like the detached head of a dreamer seeking with eyes sealed to receive the hungry lips of one summoned from some remote place." This is Miller's dreamlike prose. His obscenities insinuate themselves naturally into the web of these images. Their sulfurous *vérisme* is but the crudity of an erotic dream that ignores all boundaries and all attempts at censure: "[T]he Negress was the queen of the Harem. You had only to look at her to get an erection. Her eyes seemed to be swimming in sperm . . . Going up the narrow winding stairs behind her I couldn't resist the temptation to slide my hand up her crotch" (*Tropic of Cancer*). "The dominoes were lying all over the floor and the tablecloth was on the floor too. Suddenly Valeska was leaning against the table, her tongue halfway down my throat, my hand between her legs. As I laid her back on the table she twined her legs around me" (*Tropic of Capricorn*).

And another scene, chosen from among hundreds of candidates:

> When I got home my wife was awake and sore as hell because I had stayed out so long. We had a hot discussion and finally I lost my temper and I clouted her and she fell on the floor and began to weep and sob and then the kid woke up and hearing the wife bawling she got frightened and began to scream at the top of her lungs. The girl upstairs came running down to see what was the matter. She was in her kimono and her hair was hanging down her back . . . We put the wife to bed with a wet towel around her forehead and while the girl upstairs was bending over I stood behind her and lifting her kimono I got it into her and she stood there a long time talking a lot of foolish, soothing nonsense." (*Tropic of Capricorn*)

Miller insists that he wrote many of his priapic scenes in a sort of waking dream, under the dictates of a Voice that could be so despotic that Miller felt he should release himself from any responsibility; he had after all, written against his will, as this passage from *Big Sur and the Oranges of Hieronymus Bosch* testifies:

> When I began the Interlude called "The Land of Fuck" — meaning "Cockaigne" — I couldn't believe my ears. "*What's that?*" I cried, never dreaming of what I was

being led into. "Don't ask me to put *that* down, please. You're only creating more trouble for me." But my pleas were ignored. Sentence by sentence I wrote it down, having not the slightest idea what was to come next. Reading copy the following day — it came in installments — I would shake my head and mutter like a lost one. Either it was sheer drivel and hogwash or it was sublime. In any case, I was the one who had to sign his name to it. How could I possibly imagine then that some few years later a judicial triumvirate, eager to prove me a sinner, would accuse me of having written such passages "for gain." Here I was begging the Muse *not* to get me into trouble with the powers that be, *not* to make me write out all those "filthy" words, all those scandalous, scabrous lines, pointing out in that deaf and dumb language which I employed when dealing with the Voice that soon, like Marco Polo, Cervantes, Bunyan *et alii*, I would have to write my books in jail or at the foot of the gallows . . .

★   ★   ★

Miller always felt that his texts had a holy aura and were shrouded in sanctity. What was he but a mere scribe to a higher power? How could he presume to judge anything he'd written, or alter anything? Like Victor Hugo, who was also hesitant about going back and second-guessing himself, Miller felt that he didn't have the right to add or remove parts of his work. Even the flattest of passages might contain the breath of the Other, the inchoate could conceal the sublime, the superb might have been swept up in the gutter, like a diamond in a torrent of mud and silt. Therein also lies his justification, he says, for his lack of self-critical judgment, his refusal to evaluate his own works.

In these passages dictated by the Voice, Miller was practicing the kind of "automatic writing" advocated by the

Surrealists, to whom he felt kinship. He especially admired André Breton's *Nadja* — perhaps, again, because of the main character's resemblance to June — which enchanted and disoriented him. He believed it to be one of the "strangest" books of its period. But Miller could also be very hard on the Surrealists. Solitary wolf that he was, he criticized them for doing everything as a pack and making too much of a fuss about it. Their insanity was a little too clean, he felt; they mobilized all the conscious powers so that they could flesh out the unconscious. At bottom, they were inoffensive revolutionaries — paper tigers — always harping on the word *revolution*, while also leading a comfortable life. They might have wanted to shake up the order of society, but they wanted to do so without taking too many risks, and especially without running afoul of the law, the way Villon, Rabelais, the Marquis de Sade, Baudelaire, Flaubert, and others had done. Miller knew whereof he spoke, because no one had opened as dangerously wide the doors to the underground life as he, oblivious of the hue and cry that would ensue. Compared with the risks that Miller ran, the Surrealist poets were as prim as choirboys. In the end they were prisoners to an aesthetic.

Miller told me that when the Surrealists and Dadaism were in vogue in the twenties, he knew nothing about them. When he got to meet them ten years later, he realized that he had himself been one without having realized it. He was never much interested in doctrines; if anything, they inspired him to seek his own path. Still, like the Surrealists and the Dadaists, Henry believed that dreams provided fertile soil for writing, and that writing did involve the struggle to bring to the surface that which was unknown, hidden, and unrealized. But he only employed Surrealist techniques when it felt natural and spontaneous to do so, and not because he wanted to be counted as one of their adherents. He thought that "automatic writing" was both too deliberate and too aimless. No writer can renounce meaning and significance; even when he is being obscure, the writer must try to remain intelligible. The only thing he wrote that he thought was like what the Surrealists were doing was "Into the Night Life."

Miller had his own views about the reasons for the Surrealist phenomenon. As a movement, he once explained to me, it could have originated only in France, because basically it was a reaction against the rigor and rationality of French thinking. However much they were aware of it or not, the French were Cartesians, not given to the magical, the irrational, or the absurd. With Shakespeare, Swift, Sterne, Lewis Carroll — whom Miller adored, once telling me that he would have given his right arm to have written Carroll's books — the English had proved they were at home in dream worlds and could accept the strange, the unconscious, the nonsensical. So too the Germans, with their great Romantic poets Hölderlin, Novalis, Brentano, and Jean Paul. The Americans as well, with Melville, Edgar Allan Poe — who was a kind of Surrealist, after all — and the madcap comedy of Mack Sennett, Buster Keaton, the Marx Brothers, vaudeville, and the music hall. France was alone in needing a Surrealist movement.

Interestingly, thirty years later, the critic Jean Starobinski would come to the same conclusion. Here is what he wrote about André Breton just after Breton's death:

> In its radicalness, this skepticism (regarding any representations and ideas taken for granted) is easily the equal to Descartes' hyperbolic doubt, aside from the fact that the *before* and the *after* of Cartesian doubt are rigorously reversed: it is no longer a matter of hunting down the dream or the fragment of a dream in order to reconstruct

the world rationally, but rather of destroying the very world that reason has built, in order to open the field to dreams, even to evil spirits, both restored to the ontological dignity of which Descartes stripped them. Descartes banned the occult qualities of magic from the world in order to replace it with technology and science (in which everything happens though numbers and laws); Breton went in the opposite direction, pointing the world away from the technical and back toward the magical, back toward the omnipotence of desire . . . On this *tabula rasa*, this wood surface so polished that it becomes a magic mirror, all the creatures of the fantastic, and all the fabulous fruits of the golden ages and paradises lost, are born again. ("L'Autorité suprême" ["The Supreme Authority"], *La Nouvelle Revue Française*)

Miller's storytelling was really nothing more or less than the creative gift of a visionary. His genius was in being able to lie as easily as breathe. He could start with the real and transform it into whatever he wanted. In 1964, when Henry informed me how suprised he was by the precision and authenticity of what I had recorded in my book *Conversations with Picasso*, he also told me that as far the conversations in his own work went, they were "trickeries and inventions from beginning to end." "*Lucky you*," I replied to him in a letter, "who've never had to take notes. You haven't needed to! *Lucky you*, who could make up all dialogue in your work and replace a defective memory with imagination. *Lucky you! Lucky you!* I live in what I see and hear, whereas your treasures are buried deep within yourself, deep within the bowels of your inner self, and from them you can bring forth copper, or silver, or gold. If you hadn't been able to make things up and mobilize your imaginative faculties, you would never have been able to mine those treasures."

As for myself, I believe that Henry Miller, this "pathological liar," this "pornographer," was a poet, a great lyric poet, even though he never wrote (that I am aware of) more than one or two poems using a metrical pattern. The great masses of his prose — except when it gets a little dry, as when his Puritan side begins to produce metaphysical rhetoric — reveal the plentifully rich veins of a poetry unhindered by strictures, whether metric or rhythmic. Miller's poetry lies within his prose. To find it, all you need do is transcribe his sentences as blank verse. Here are several examples taken at random from his work:

Renée Tietjen

She was leaning on the iron fence
beside the gate
and the wind molded her thin silk dress
about her limbs.
. . . .
All light and grace,
chaste,
seductive,
with golden tresses and sea-green eyes.
Always silent,
always seraphic.
Buffeted by the wind,
she swayed back and forth
like a young willow.
Her breasts,
which were two nubile hemispheres,
and the little tuft
which adorned the pelvis,
seemed extraordinarily alive and sensitive.
They met the wind
like the bulging contour
of a ship's prow.
. . . .

Now and then the wind lifted her skirt
and we gasped
when we caught sight
of the milky flesh above her knees.

(*Plexus*)

The Heat in Nevada

The heat was rippling up slant-wise,
like Jacob's Ladder
seen through a corrugated mirror.

The sun had become
a gory omelette
frying itself to a crisp . . .

The engine boiling in its oil
like an antique instrument,
the tires expanding like dead toads,
the nuts falling out like old teeth . . .
My brain-pan was vaporized.

It was sizzling outdoors.

The street was just a
fried banana
flaming with rum and creosote.

The houses were wilting,
sagging to their knees,
threatening to melt
into glue or glucose.

(*The Air-Conditioned Nightmare*)

I Believe

I believe in God the Father,
in Jesus Christ his only begotten Son,
in the blessed Virgin Mary,
the Holy Ghost,
in Adam Cadmium,
in chrome nickel,
the oxides and mercurochromes,
in waterfowls and water cress,
in epileptoid seizures,
in bubonic plagues,
in devachan,
in planetary conjunctions,
in chicken tracks
and stick-throwing,
in revolutions,
in stock crashes,
in wars,
earthquakes,
cyclones,
in Kali Yuga
and in hula-hula.
I believe.
I believe.

(*Sexus*)

Finally, this "poem" about Lucienne on the sidewalks of Montmartre:

Lucienne

I think of Lucienne
sailing down the boulevard
with her wings outstretched,

THE "VOICE"

a huge silver condor
suspended over the sluggish tide
of traffic,
a strange bird
from the tips of the Andes
with a rose-white belly
and a tenacious little knob.

(Tropic of Cancer)

XIV

The Delicious Rogue

Henry's primary victim, and the one who also should have been the first to be revolted by all the lies Miller wrote about him, was Henry Miller himself. His Madame Bovary-like self-centered restlessness makes him an ideal character, though also one trapped in his own odious dissoluteness, an abject figure who indulges in the imbecilic and idiotic. He takes sensual delight in the whole range of his reprehensible actions. The whole point is to scandalize the reader, to make him cry out in indignation, the way one of his characters does in *Plexus*, "You're ashamed of your better self, if I may put it that way. You'd rather be thought wicked than good." And indeed Miller never wanted to seem better than he was; he preferred to malign himself, horrified that he might be mistaken for a model of virtue. Autobiography automatically engenders this kind of distortion. "Whoever writes a confession," says Goethe, "runs the risk of appearing pathetic, because one always confesses disease and sin and one never professes one's virtues." "I have always been more attracted by hell than by heaven," he told Georges Belmont. (As Aragon once said, "I prefer the Devil to God.") In a letter to me dated September 1964, Miller wrote, "In the trilogy of The Rosy Crucifixion, I deliberately tried to make myself more stupid than I probably was or am." More than stupid, he wanted to make himself appear downright dastardly.

Scenes in which he comes across as the bad guy abound in his work, whether or not they have any basis in the truth. In *Plexus*, for example, he recounts how, for no particularly good reason, he abused and humiliated a poor old man:

> I don't know what possessed me, but before I could check myself I was making sport of the poor devil, baiting him with questions which he couldn't answer, examining the shoelaces minutely, stuffing a cigar in his mouth, and in general behaving like a cad and an idiot. Everyone looked at me in amazement, and finally with stern disapproval. The old man was in tears.

He also seems proud of begging, stealing, and defrauding people, particularly if the victim is blind, old, or a pregnant woman. He boasts about having stolen money from a blind newspaper vendor to buy a subway ticket. At the end of *Tropic of Cancer*, when his friend Fillmore sneaks off to the United States, leaving Henry at the Gare Saint-Lazare with 2,500 francs to give to Ginette, Fillmore's pregnant French mistress, Miller, naturally, keeps the money for himself: "Ginette need never know what had happened," Henry reasons cold-bloodedly. "And even if she did learn that he had left her 2,500 francs or so she couldn't prove it." Earlier in the novel, a girl agrees to take him to her place for one hundred francs. Early the next morning, while he's getting ready to slip out before she wakes, he decides to take the hundred francs back. She had put them away in her purse, which she's stuck way up on the top shelf of the armoire. Miller takes the money and departs on tiptoe. Having been taken in for the night by a homosexual, he finds it completely natural to decamp at dawn with a copy of Joyce's *Ulysses* under his arm. He also decides he might as well go through the man's wallet. In *Plexus* he proudly recounts how he and June left without paying from a North Carolina hotel, whose owner had been putting them up and feeding them for several months.

Despite his dissolute lifestyle, Miller is still capable of feeling tenderness, or at least pity, toward his first wife, yet these fine sentiments hardly prevent him from being unfaithful to her under the conjugal roof. One night he brings home a seventeen-year-old girl, and debates whether or not to make love with her, not out of scruple, but from fear that his wife will find them. "We stood there a long while embracing each other and then I thought to myself no, it's a crime, and besides maybe the wife didn't go to the movies at all, maybe she'll be ducking back any minute" (*Tropic of Capricorn*). So as not to be taken by surprise, he deems it more prudent to take the young girl to a deserted beach. Sometimes, though very rarely, a glimmer of remorse awakens him to the idea that he has committed some act of villainy, such as when he puts some extra money into the cup of a blind newspaper vendor from whom he'd stolen. Though Miller portrayed me as a pornographer in *Tropic of Cancer*, his intention was not to debase me; it was to debase himself.

Whenever someone innocently said that he admired the sympathetic way Henry listened to poor fools, and that it brought out what was best in him and most interesting about the people he talked to, he would protest, loudly, that he always exaggerated the worst qualities of the people he despised. And if some naive reader ventured to suggest that they found no trace of malice in his work, Miller would reply that, on the contrary he always caricatured maliciously the people he didn't like. He tells us in his study of Rimbaud, *The Time of the Assassins*, that he was delighted when he learned that the young Rimbaud signed his letters "The Heartless Rimbaud." "Heartless was an adjective I was fond of hearing applied to myself. I had no principles, no loyalty, no code whatsoever; when it suited me, I could be thoroughly unscrupulous, with friend and foe alike. I usually repaid kindness with insult and injury. I was insolent, arrogant, intolerant, violently prejudiced, relentlessly obstinate." He wrote Durrell that he had no close friends and that in fact he was a "sort of monster." People would attach themselves to him and when he'd had enough of them he would drop them. "I never helped any one expecting that it would do any good," he says in *Tropic of Capricorn*. "I helped because I was helpless to do otherwise." Some people feel that he placed feeling above intelligence — after all, did he not write a book titled *The Wisdom of the Heart*? Yet for Miller the heart has nothing to do with goodness, charity, or generosity; it has to do with emotion and lust. The heart is not a moral entity, but a muscle that nourishes the guts and the sexual organs.

An example of Miller's "charity" can be found in his conversations with his friend Belmont. One evening, Henry invited a bum to sit at their table at the Dôme. The man began to pour out his heart and tell his tale of woe. Miller listened silently for an hour, then told the man that the best thing he could do was go and throw himself into the Seine. As soon as someone, even a nobody like this poor bum, captured his attention, Miller's nostrils dilated like those of a famished animal. He smelled meat. He knew how to talk to people, especially rogues, shysters, liars, and prostitutes, and he attracted them as much as he was attracted by them. It had been that way since his childhood: "As a mere lad — in the old neighborhood — I had been accustomed to mixing with half-wits, incipient gangsters, petty crooks, would-be prize fighters, epileptics, drunks and sluts. Everyone in that dear ancient neighborhood was a 'character'" (*Plexus*). With his false air of sympathy — like the wolf in "Little Red Riding Hood" — Miller would listen while people gave him the stories of their lives, with all of their sins and crimes, only interrupting to add his "hum hums," rumblings of encouragement, sympathy, and surprise. The more dramatic someone's life story got, the more it got his engines going. He would rub his hands in glee. A willing victim! We have, among others, that supposed murderer he met on a train during a trip across the United States, who told him everything, and that "desert rat" whose confession he listened to at the edge of the Grand Canyon. One of his victims was a man named Max, who, when he saw Henry's tender, caring look, fell right into the trap. He believed Henry was actually interested in him, and wanted to help him out of his misery. Fool! Miller only wanted his story. With his customary bluntness, Miller sizes up his own intentions:

> That's it for Max. Max is a *monsieur* for the moment. He's looking at me with that wan smile again. Well, *courage*, Max! To-day I'm going to lift you to heaven — and then drop you like a sinker! Jesus, just one more day I'll waste on this bastard and then bango! I'll put the skids under him. To-day I'm going to listen to you, you bugger . . . listen to every nuance. I'll extract the last drop of juice — and then, *overboard you go!* ("Max")

In his desire to reveal openly how vile he was, Miller was no doubt deeply influenced by the example of Rimbaud. The author of the *Bateau ivre* constantly drew attention to the evil side of his character, even to underline it in red and boast about playing the heavy. But it was to the teachings of John Cowper Powys, the venerated master, that Miller listened most closely. Powys inspired him to follow the path of masochistic self-punishment and self-humiliation. Powys had been fond of denigrating himself, thinking of himself as asocial, morbid, and driven by sadistic tendencies. Miller recognized this. "Like Céline," he wrote with admiration in "Living Books," "he can speak of himself in the most derogatory terms, call himself a fool, a clown, a weakling, a coward, a degenerate, even a 'sub-human' being, without in the least diminishing his stature." One cannot talk about about Miller's egoism and insensitivity without doing so in the context of his tendency to make things up. His insensitivity really was nothing more than the natural by-product of his writerly sensibility. For the devouring appetite of a full-blown flesh-eater, everything becomes raw material: books, meetings, trips, loves, family, everything. In order to be a writer, Miller felt he had to achieve the otherworldliness of the Buddha, to which all of his life he aspired in vain.

Like the great masters, who often placed a portrait of themselves in their paintings, Miller put himself in his essay "The Immorality of Morality." Though the portrait is supposedly anonymous, the "delicious rogue" so completely wrapped up in himself is none other than the author of *Tropic of Cancer*:

> He does nothing for the world, and very little for himself. He simply enjoys life, taking it as he finds it. Naturally he works as little as possible; naturally he takes no concern for the morrow. Without making a fetish of it, he takes inordinately good care of himself, being moderate in all things and showing discrimination with respect to everything that demands his time or attention. He is a

connoisseur of food and wine who is never in danger of becoming a glutton or a drunkard. He loves women and knows how to make them happy . . . When he's radiantly happy, and he's almost always happy, he sometimes loves himself so much, is so delighted with his own happiness, so to speak, that he will kiss himself — on the hand or arm, whichever is most convenient. I believe he would kiss his own ass, if he could, in certain moments of exaltation.

Why would Miller want the world to see him as a rogue? Because he doesn't want to play the game. Because he gets a kick out of life and can't bring himself to dwell on its miseries. Some wondered if he wasn't being spineless or playing the fool. Why didn't he defend himself? they wondered. How is it possible to indulge in the sins of the flesh with so light a heart and seem to suffer not one whit from guilt? "What health and vitality, what joy, radiates from his countenance! It's almost shameful to look that way in a world such as ours. And when he kisses himself all over, because the meal was good and he enjoyed it so much, he seems to be thanking the Creator in dog-like fashion. But if it be dog-like, his behavior, it is without a doubt meritorious. Would that we were all more dog-like!"

★　　　★　　　★

Miller's penchant for exaggeration can also be found in his moods; he was either deliriously happy or deeply depressed. He himself recognized this. His horoscope had told him early on that his magnetism would carry with it bouts of depression, and indeed moments of exuberant exaltation and morbid melancholy alternate in him with unnerving swiftness.

He had both "delusions of grandeur" and "delusions of

debasement." Miller could happily acquiesce when some-one called him the new Christ or Buddha, the great Mystic of the East, a new religious leader, a genius of the caliber of Rabelais or Shakespeare, and he didn't protest when Durrell wrote that he thought Miller one of the greats. Miller himself had his moments of euphoria, such as after he'd written something that really pleased him and he could imagine that his work would still be around in the year 5000.

At other moments, grandiosity would give way to the feeling that he was a failure, a failure as a man and a failure as a writer. "I'm lying on the iron bed thinking what a zero I have become, what a cipher, what a nullity, when bango! out pops the word: NONENTITY" (*Tropic of Cancer*). A quarter of a century later, he would write Durrell from Big Sur:

> I'm going through some sort of crisis. Never felt more desolate. Yet underneath very hopeful. Two nights ago I got up in the middle of the night with the firm intent of destroying everything — but it was too big a job... I seem to feel that all I have done is to create a booby-hatch. Now I can throw the letters away without replying. It's easy. The next step is to throw myself away. That's harder. One thing seems certain — that I've built on sand. Nothing I've done has any value or meaning for me any longer. I'm not an utter failure, but close to it. Time to take a new tack. Years of struggle, labor, patience, perse-verance have yielded nothing solid. I'm just where I was at the beginning — which is nowhere.

The feeling that he was a "failure," "pathetic," a "noth-ing," an "idiot," sometimes pushed him to the point of suicide, even toward embracing the idea of total annihilation — no memories, no traces — of the sort that German Nouveau, who was so dear to the Surrealists, had dreamed: to vaporize self and possessions along with all manuscripts and publications. "I wanted to be soaked through and through, then stabbed, then thrown into the gutter, then flattened out by a heavy truck, then ground down into the muck and mire, obliterated, annihilated for good and all" (*Plexus*).

Feelings of failure can save you if that failure is measured by society, rather than against childhood dreams. Miller could only measure success against the grandeur of those dreams. To have aimed too high, I believe, was the cause of Henry Miller's despair. Even into his eighties, when he was at the height of his renown, he could still boast to Belmont, "I often ask myself if I haven't been a failure. My opinion is that I've been a failure for most of my life. And still am today."

XV

Parisian Friendships

Miller came to Paris ten years too late to be part of the Lost Generation (though he was older than Pearl Buck and James Joyce). He knew none of its *monstres sacrés*, apart from William Saroyan, at least so far as I am aware. He didn't hang around Shakespeare and Company, Sylvia Beach's famous Left Bank bookstore, where he might have run into the likes of Dos Passos, Joyce, Steinbeck, and maybe Faulkner; nor did he frequent Gertrude Stein's circle, or Hemingway's fiefdom, or the Ritz, or the fashion salons, or Maxim's, or Longchamp, or any of the palaces dotting the Côte d'Azur that were so familiar to Scott Fitzgerald. Moreover, he had no desire to do so. "Aldous Huxley, Gertrude Stein, Sinclair Lewis, Hemingway, Dos Passos, Dreiser, etc., etc.," he wrote in "A Saturday Afternoon," one of the essays in *Black Spring*. "I hear no bell ringing inside me when I bring these birds to the water closet. I pull the chain and down the sewer they go." Miller was more interested in the French, and in the works of Céline, André Breton, Giono, and others. Only later, in New York, did he meet up with one of his favorite American writers, Sherwood Anderson, with whom he happened to be staying at the same hotel. Miller greatly admired Anderson's style and work, reproaching him only for his unreserved love of America.

It was from Emerson and Thoreau that he learned to rebel against social and religious institutions that limit the power of men, institutions that keep men from living life as intensely as possible. Of all American writers, Miller most fervently admired Walt Whitman. Whitman, he thought, possessed the largest and most generous vision, and had the poetic power to embrace every creature with equal tenderness and compassion. The author of *Leaves of Grass* taught him to find the great miracle of life in its daily and ordinary details. Jack London was another favorite, both as writer and revolutionary, For Melville, however, he felt no affinity. He could never even bring himself to read *Moby Dick*. He outright detested the "angel of the bizarre," Edgar Allan Poe, with his "macabre visions and crow cries," and thought Poe's stories of sleepwalkers and houses fraught with diabolical traps, his tales in which the human soul is broken and tortured, were "putrid." How, he wondered, could a spirit as delicate as Baudelaire's have loved them so?

Among the modern writers, Miller's particular bête noire was Ernest Hemingway. He thought Hemingway was a phony, a gutless coward compelled by weak nerves to turn to violence, the way others turn to drugs or madness. He hated Hemingway's two-fisted, bravado brawling side, the pose of the *aficionado* — hunter of wild beasts, fisher of sharks, bandoliered soldier heading into battle. Propped up by the myths perpetuated by the media, Hemingway was nothing more than a bully, thought Miller, and felt no admiration for Hemingway's "stenographic" style, in which reality is "traced by the eye alone in the absence of the brain."

Hemingway committed suicide at nearly the same time Céline died, and Henry wrote me in July of 1961 to say that "Céline death touched me more than Hemingway's. The latter's work never attracted me neither as a writer nor as a man. It was all just a legend created around his name."

As for James Joyce, Miller found him "too literary" for his tastes, even though there are of course plenty of affinities between them. Like Miller, Joyce lived off his friends for quite some time, and his relationship with Harriet Weaver was not unlike Miller's with Anaïs Nin. Also, like Miller, Joyce sought to represent the whole spectrum of human behavior, even the basest parts, without worrying about what people would think. His goal, like Henry's, was the unadorned truth, total honesty, and he could just as easily have been the author of this quote from *Tropic of Cancer* as Miller: "The wallpaper with which the men of science have covered the world of reality is falling to tatters. The grand whorehouse which they have made of life requires no decoration; it is essential only that the drains function adequately." And one hears Miller in those famous lines from *Portait of the Artist as a Young Man*: "I will not serve that in which I no longer believe whether it call itself my home, my fatherland or my church: and I will try to express myself in some mode of life or art as freely as I can and as wholly as I can, using for my defence the only arms I allow myself to use — silence, exile, and cunning." Miller's work, like Joyce's, was considered obscene, lubricious, indecent, and repugnant, and had been subject to the same scornful dismissal. The New York censor and the Folkestone customs agent had seized and burned as many copies of *Ulysses* as of *Tropic of Cancer*. There were other affinities: both were voluntary exiles from their native lands, and Joyce was as harsh about Ireland as Miller was about America — and as nostalgic.

It was to John Cowper Powys that Miller felt closest kinship. He thought Powys one of the truly great writers of his time. In his youth, Miller had attended several lectures Powys gave, and saw in this man of enormous and disconcerting complexity a soul akin to his own. Powys was a man riven with contradictions: peace-loving yet haunted by sadistic tendencies, cruel and also full of pity, asocial and yet a friend to humble folk, a sensualist who inclined toward the ascetic. He was, in short, quite a piece of work. But Miller's conception of love chimed with that of Powys, who cherished the acts of the flesh over sentimental attachments and believed in an eroticism freed of complicated responsibilities and tragic jealousies: To enjoy as much as possible the pleasures of the flesh, without causing harm to anyone, was his creed. Miller also agreed with Powys that reality was only real insofar as it was ruled and ruled absolutely by the mind and by the imagination, which transform reality freely, re-creating it, destroying it, turning it into myth and legend. After the war, Henry went to visit him in Stratford-on-Avon, during a trip he had planned to pay homage to Shakespeare.

★   ★   ★

But the writer to whom Henry felt the most kinship of all — and his favorite author during his Paris years — was D. H. Lawrence. Curious indeed that *Lady Chatterley's Lover* happened to appear in 1928, at the very moment Miller arrived in Europe for the first time, and that Lawrence died in March 1930, several days after Henry's return to Paris. Miller's desire to immerse himself totally in a fundamental reality, fleshly, awash in sexuality, attracted him to Lawrence, who was in many ways a much less liberated man. Indeed, Lawrence's work is imbued with a puritanism, a dolorous romanticism, particularly evident in the cult of mystery with which he shrouded sex: "Sex should come upon us as a terrible thing of suffering and privilege and mystery" wrote Lawrence in "The Birth of Sex," which Miller quotes in his essay on Lawrence, "Shadowy Monomania." "The mystery, the terror, and the tremendous power of sex should never be explained away." "The mystery must remain in its dark secrecy, and its dark, powerful dynamism." If sex was everything to Lawrence, to Miller it was only a part of life; and if Lawrence developed a mysterious religion around it, Miller saw in it only a transient passion whose role was relative. Yet, though Miller had rejected the cult of sex and, instead, wanted to demystify it by flashing obscenities in the face of respectability and prudishness, Lawrence's thinking continued to have a hold over him. Miller wanted to embrace it, if only because by so doing he might free himself of the man to whom he sometimes referred as an "incubus" and a "little midget," and called "intolerant and mean." He nearly calls Lawrence a hypocrite: "Just as he glorifies life, in order to slay it through his art, so he glorifies woman in order to execrate her, punish her, for the necessitous character of her role, which he recognizes only too clearly." Miller also reproached Lawrence (who died in Vence) for his hatred of the French, for seeing them as decadent rather than as men of flesh and blood who loved life and breath.

Miller had intended to write a short essay on Lawrence, and when his publisher asked him for a sixty-page pamphlet on the writer, he set to work on it. What he had in mind was a single "philosophical" work, of a piece with his spontaneous, autobiographical narratives, and he even hoped it would come out before *Tropic of Cancer.* Miller was too impulsive and intuitive to write a serious work of scholarship, but he launched full-steam into the project, determined to take on and explicate with clarity all of Lawrence's ideas, even those with contradictions that defied comprehension. "The notes are piling up around me like weeds," Miller noted. He labored for two years on the work, accumulating a vast pile of notes: "By the time I had written a hundred pages I was so deep in the study of Lawrence's work that I could no longer see the forest for the trees," he wrote Pierre Lesdain. In the end he could not clear a trail through the jungle of notes that had grown up around him. He wrote Anaïs in February 1934 that, in an "act of heroism" he had destroyed it. Only a small fragment of *The World of Lawrence* was ever published.

★　　★　　★

Among those anglophone writers that Miller knew in Paris, I must mention Michael Fraenkel first. Fraenkel lived in studio number 18, on the ground floor of Villa Seurat, but Henry had known him since 1930, when Fraenkel had sheltered Miller during his hobo days. His Trotsky-like mustache gave him the air of a Russian revolutionary, but he was a man of leisure, having made a fortune with his books (he also played the stock market with some success), and so could devote himself to his passion: philosophy. Fraenkel was a man of ideas, an intellectual through and through, and the author of an elegant book about death, prefaced by Miller, titled *Bastard Death*. Fred called him a "mortician," and Henry said to him, "With every line you write and every word you utter, you plant death!" Much separated these two men, who nonetheless would stay up all night locked in fierce debate. A believer in instinct, in flesh, blood, and vitals, Henry did not have too elevated an opinion of "thinking," and even less of "thinkers," yet he also secretly dreamed of being included in their ranks. Fraenkel's mania for analyzing everything exasperated Miller, and yet there was something that attracted him — Fraenkel was a good punching bag, a way for Miller to vent his spleen. Fraenkel recognized Miller's originality and genius, but thought that he was going down the wrong road. *Tropic of Cancer*, from his point of view, was a "repugnant and sordid dunghill." He wanted to convince Henry that, way down deep, he was a thinker, and that if he denied this in himself, if he turned his back on thinking and spat upon it, it was because of what America had done to him. That was why, on the terrace of the Brasserie Zeyer one evening, Fraenkel proposed that they exchange letters one thousand words in length on the subject of *Hamlet*, the most enigmatic of all works of literature. Miller accepted the challenge. In an interminable exchange of correspondence, the two men plumbed Hamlet's character, from the ramparts of Elsinore to the psychiatrist's office. What went on in the Dane's mind? Revenge disguised as madness? Was he truly mad, or pretending? Insensitive or ultrasensitive? Sincere, or lacking sincerity? A nervous wreck or a man of action? To Henry, *Hamlet* was a tragedy about cowardice, frustration, and impotence; the disease that eats at him is nothing but the hypertropic madness of thought and conscience. As a contrast to *Hamlet*, Miller proposes the robust, Dionysiac health of life — music, dance, ecstasy. To Fraenkel, *Hamlet* was the key to the symbolic vaults of western civilization, dominated as it is by conscious thought. He saw Hamlet as the first western man to analyze his ills, embodying the victory of thought over action and feeling.

★   ★   ★

Miller met the writer and journalist Wambly Bald at the Dôme. Though Bald was one of Montparnasse's most nonchalant-acting characters, he actually sweated blood

trying to pick up gossip about American artists for his col-
umn in the *Chicago Herald Tribune*, "La Vie de bohème."
Around the typewriter in his hotel room were scattered
hundreds of crumpled-up balls of paper; the paper in the
typewriter usually had only one or two sentences typed on it.
"It's the first sentence that counts," Bald told me. "The
others will follow like sheep. But I sometimes have to go
through dozens of sheets of paper before I find that first
sentence." From time to time, to pay Bald back for buying
him dinner, Henry would give him a hand in writing his
gossip. By way of thanks, Bald devoted one of his columns to
Miller, the unknown writer so rich with promise. Bald asked
me if I would do a sketch of Miller to accompany the article,
which appeared on October 14, 1931. It was the first piece
ever to be written about Henry, and it was balm to his soul.
My caricature, signed "Brassaï," pictured Miller sitting at
the Dôme in his rumpled hat. As a joke, I drew a bottle of
champagne plunked down before him on the table. He used
the picture in several of his books. As for Wambly Bald, he
left Paris when the *Tribune* closed down.

★   ★   ★

Henry knew several English and American writers who published a literary review in Paris. In 1931, at the request of
Paul Eliot and Eugene Jolas, the editorial director of *Transition*, Miller's first piece, "The Médrano Circus," was published, soon followed by a piece about the Six Days [a
bicycle race]. He also worked on the *New Review*, published
by the literary critic Samuel Putnam. Putnam, the author of a
book on Rabelais that Miller much admired, had spent a
dozen years in Paris. In the second issue of the magazine,
Henry published "Buñuel, or, Thus Cometh to End Everywhere the Golden Age." Thunderstruck by Buñuel's film,

Henry was delighted to have found another brother-in-arms and was thrilled to have met him. Anaïs, who had not yet met Miller, read his piece in the *New Review,* and noted in her *Diary:* "The other day Richard [Osborn] brought me an article by Miller on the Golden Age. It was as effective as a bomb. It reminded me of Lawrence's 'I am a human bomb.' In these pages there is a savage and primitive quality and compared to everything else I've read it's a jungle. The article is short, but the words fall like hatchets, exploding with hate. I thought I heard African drums in the Jardins des Tuileries."

In the third issue of the *New Review,* published in August 1931, Miller's first short story, "Mademoiselle Claude," appeared. In the same issue were pictures of sculptures by Arp and Henry Moore, and two of my own photographs, the first ones ever to be published, I believe. In the table of contents of this issue were Miguel de Unamuno, Ezra Pound, Alfred Perlès, Wembly Bald, and, interestingly, Samuel Beckett, who contributed a poem called "Return to the Vestry," which ran on two pages. Later, in 1937 or 1938, Miller met Beckett and reproached him, somewhat crudely it would seem, for having fallen too much under the influence of Joyce. But until *Murphy,* who would have seen Beckett as the author of *Waiting for Godot?* Fifteen years later, Henry attended a performance of that play at the Babylone Theater, and was overwhelmed. When next he saw Beckett, he rushed up to him, kissed him, and called him a genius.

Finally, in the twenty-seventh issue of *Transition,* in 1937, Miller published "The Cosmological Eye," an essay on the painter Hans Reichel. I should also mention another friend, an editor by the name of Edward Titus, the husband of Helena Rubinstein, who had a bookstore on Boulevard Montparnasse and was publishing a literary magazine called *This Quarter.* Henry had several pieces published in it, but under the pseudonym Valentin Nieting, the name of his German grandfather, born around 1850, who had deserted the Prussian army and emigrated to the United States.

In December 1937, Miller began working on a French literary review called *Volonté*, published by George Belmont, alias Georges Pelorson. Through Raymond Queneau, Belmont had met Miller and was able to get hold of the unpublished epilogue to *Black Spring*, an epilogue that was not included in the final version. "I was Miller's first translator," Belmont boasted to me once. The piece appeared in the first issue Winter 1937. Other pieces followed.

"I was at the time in very close contact with Henry," Belmont recalled, "and when he left for Greece, he left his books and drawings with me. There was even a very pretty painting by Reichel. Unfortunately, all of his affairs, along with a packet of Miller's letters, remained in the possession of my first wife, who didn't want to give them up. My only regret is that I never knew either Fraenkel or Durrell. The latter had just left Paris when I met Miller."

★   ★   ★

Among all the classic French writers, Miller placed Rabelais on the highest pedestal (he even figures with Cervantes, Swift, and Goethe, Miller's "four horsemen of the Apocalypse"). Behind Rabelais came Montaigne, who Miller thought was "completely exceptional in French culture," someone who knew how to align his thought with life. In Montaigne, Miller saw a distant kindred spirit. Was it not Montaigne who wrote, "I despise a peevish and sad spirit that slides over life's pleasures . . . For myself, I am bound to say all that I dare to reveal, even those thoughts that are unpublishable. The worst of my actions and conditions seem to me not so ugly as I find it ugly and cowardly not to acknowledge them" (*Essays*, Book III). If Miller admired Balzac and his work, there was no love. Aside from *Louis Lambert* and *Séraphita*, none of Balzac's works seized his imagination.

And he could never bring himself to read either Stendhal or Restif de la Bretonne, though the author of *Paris Nights* had much in common with Miller, as Miller himself acknowledged. Each time I mentioned that to him, he would reply that it was simply not possible to know any writer who had left behind five hundred volumes. Miller tried to read the Marquis de Sade, but the works just didn't hold his attention. He was not interested in perversion.

The writer he revered most of all, the brightest star in the "glittering constellations of French writers," was Arthur Rimbaud, with whom Miller first became acquainted when he was thirty-six years old and living in his New York basement. It was love at first read. There was no need to understand French, or to use a dictionary, because, he wrote in "Remember to Remember," "It is not French one needs to know but the forgotten tongue of the poet. Rimbaud is the last of the line and the first of a new order for which there is no name." It seemed to Miller that Rimbaud had a divine side, and it was that divinity he wanted to match, and if possible to surpass. Rimbaud's spell was so strong that it inspired Miller to write lines from his works in chalk on walls, even outer walls. Rimbaud was a mirror in which he saw his own image. "Nothing he says is alien to me, however wild, absurd or difficult to understand" (*The Time of the Assassins*). Miller shared with Rimbaud the feeling that he would never find his place in the scheme of things, that he would never have an occupation. They shared hatreds: of all supposedly "honest" work, of the places of their birth, of their mothers (like Miller's mother, Madame Rimbaud was cold, rancorous, and puritan). Like Rimbaud, Miller had made his attempts at escape, experienced the shameful returns home, and longed for exotic countries. "I choose Rimbaud because through him, through his break with the whole set-up, I understand France best. With his own youthful hands he created a monument as lasting as the great cathedrals" ("Remember to Remember"). Rimbaud's genius awed him so that he believed that had he read Rimbaud in his youth, he never would have written a thing.

Another French writer that Miller placed among the first ranks was Elie Faure. Henry was only twenty years old when Faure's *History of Art* was published in New York in 1912, and the book made a deep impression on him. He could recite entire passages by heart. Through his whole life, Miller acknowledged his debt to this favorite writer, and his admiration was almost without bounds. Had he been brave enough, Miller wrote in *The Books in My Life*, he would have visited Faure, fallen on his knees, and kissed his hand. When he got to France, Henry was astounded to learn that Faure was nearly unknown in his own country — no street bore his name, and no one had erected a moment to this "dear Master." He also learned with surprise that if Faure hadn't practiced medicine, he might have starved to death. Faure died in Paris in 1937, at sixty-four. There were, therefore, seven years during which Miller could have knocked at Faure's door, fallen to his knees, and kissed the master's hand.

Miller discovered Jean Giono in a small book and stationery store on Rue d'Alésia. While he was browsing through the books, the owner's daughter suddenly handed him *Que ma joie demeure* [*May My Joy Remain*]. Again he was overwhelmed, enchanted by a sensual, vigorous art that provided the full spectrum of colors, smells, the textures of plants from Provence. Here, Miller told himself, was a writer who had succeeded in doing in the South of France what

Faulkner had done in the American South: carve out his own territory. In Giono's rebellion against the oppression of industrialism, in his condemnation of "modern" life, in his appeal for a return to a simpler life of arcadian bliss, and in his rustic pantheism so reminiscent of Rousseau and Thoreau, Miller believed he heard his own voice. Giono the anarchist-peasant was a comrade. They never met face-to-face. When Miller tried to visit him in Manosque, Giono was not there.

The first French writers Miller met in Paris were Blaise Cendrars and Raymond Queneau. It was 1934. Queneau had just published his first novel, *Le Chiendent* [*The Trouble*]. His second novel, *Gueule de pierre* [*Rockjaw*], shortly preceded the publication of *Tropic of Cancer*. Raymond fully appreciated Miller's originality, and Miller always took seriously what Raymond had to say. He would sometimes give Queneau copies of his manuscripts with the hope of interesting him in a French translation. Queneau had read Miller's work on Lawrence in early 1935 and found it, he said, enormously interesting, but probably not suitable for the French market. Still, given that nothing had as yet been written about Lawrence in France, he urged Miller to finish the work. Raymond was a loyal supporter of Henry's from the beginning, and wrote a glowing article about *Tropic of Cancer* and *Black Spring* in the December 1936 edition of *La Nouvelle Revue Française*. "Since *Ulysses*," he wrote, "no work of expatriation has caused such a stir as *Tropic of Cancer*, Henry Miller's first novel, like *Ulysses*, published in Paris — and for the same reasons. It is a dense and thick work, written in a language that is both violent and precise." He lavishes praise on *Black Spring* as well. "Henry Miller's verbal mastery now emerges unhindered, and his language grows in beauty. He writes with precision, power, and passion." In 1939, Queneau translated and published "Via Dieppe-Newhaven" in the journal *Mesure*.

Miller also knew Jacques Klein, a promising young playwright. It was to Jacques's brother Roger that Miller became particularly attached. "From the moment of our first meeting," Roger once told me,

> I had the impression that he would be in my life forever, and though fate separated us, I never forgot him. Henry was in a class all by himself. I never knew anyone else like him. He wasn't handsome, you know, and made no attempt to please anyone, and yet he was incredibly seductive. Just as soon as he had started to speak, if only to emit a few groans, he inspired confidence in people. He was so natural, so open. When he cast his line at night, whores and nut cases were drawn straight to him. He had the aura of a saint or a prophet, and if he'd ever had the idea of starting a sect, he could have been a billionaire, worshiped by millions of converts. His grunts carried the gospel of life. Women were irresistibly attracted to him.
>
> I often stopped by his place at the end of a long day, because it was only a few steps from my studio to Villa Seurat. One night I was feeling a little depressed and went by to see him. This happened forty years ago, but I remember it as if it were today. His fingers had not yet stopped moving along the keyboard when the eye glinted in a friendly and malicious way and the slightly gravelly voice dragged several syllables along it: "Hello Roger! *Asse-e-e-eyez vous . . . Prends donc un coup de rou-ou-ou-ou-ge!*" [Sit down and pour yourself a glass of red wine.] His voice was as hesitant and slow as his fingers were fast. "You look down, Roger. Come on. I'll take you out to a nightclub. That'll revive you."
>
> So we spent an evening at a cabaret on Rue Pigalle. At four in the morning, there were just the two of us and four hangers-on, women kneeling around Henry and listening to him in ecstasy. It didn't matter that at this point Henry was still massacring the French tongue. He made

himself understood. I often noticed this later on. The minute they looked at him, women fell at his feet, even the youngest and most beautiful among them, and even though he made no effort to please them.

The barman gave us the bill, and to my stupefaction Henry admitted that he didn't have a sou on him. I didn't either. Things didn't look good. We could have ended up getting hauled down to the police station and even put in jail. Just then the main hanger-on intervened. "Let your friend" — meaning me — "pay with a check." It was quite a favor, given that at the time no nightclub accepted personal checks. And if I hadn't had my checkbook on me, she said that she would have paid the bill herself. I had enough in my account to cover it, and this was lucky because first thing the next morning the barman went to the bank to cash it. Some guy, that Henry! Inviting me out to a nightclub and broke! Still, at bottom, he was right, you know? Broke as he was, he always seemed to find a way to live it up.

XVI

A Trip to New York

In late 1934, having been in Paris for nearly five years, though only barely installed in the Villa Seurat, Miller felt a sudden urge to return to the United States. However much he bad-mouthed America, he was also homesick, and this overwhelmed the fear he had had since the disastrous Dieppe-Newhaven trip, when he was panic-stricken that the French authorities would send him packing.

America beckoned. When in the company of other exiles from the States, he would pull out an old map of New York and reminisce about Manhattan; nostalgia would also sometimes strike when he saw an American film. When he inhaled the smell of brackish water while visiting The Hague, he was stricken with homesickness, and his thoughts were of the wide-open and savagely beautiful expanses of his homeland, still nearly untouched — the burning deserts and snow-capped peaks, those places where in the course of a single day you can experience every one of the seasons. "We were getting quite foolish about the cows and sheep and the big open spaces where men are men and all that crap. If a boat had swung along instead of the train we'd have hopped aboard and said good-bye to it all" (*Tropic of Cancer*). For all that he thanked his lucky stars that he lived in Paris, he was haunted by America.

Frank Dobo once told me that Henry might have felt no tenderness for America, but that he talked about it all the time. "And it was precisely the stories that he told me about life in America that made me want to go and live there. Now that I'm forty years older, I can better measure the degree to which Henry was American, and always was American, despite his exile." Henry once told me in California that he was "terribly American" and always had been. His productive years in France had only served to deepen his connection to America. "I'm an American who wears his Americanism like a wound," he said. F. J. Temple, one of Henry's biographers and friends, has rightly noted that being violently revolted by America is to remain American, and that Miller's curses and blasphemies are but vehement forms of nationalism. "I love it, even though I spit on it," Miller confessed, "and I love it even more by doing just that." To execrate a place with such passion is a form of inverted love.

Though he might have gotten misty-eyed at the thought that he would once again fill his lungs with New York's invigorating sea air, the true source of Miller's joy wasn't in returning to the city of his birth, but, as he writes in *Hamlet*, "my joy in realizing that I am free of this country, that I have no need of it, that I can not be dominated over or tyrannized or enslaved by it." Twenty years later, when Lawrence Durrell wrote in his introduction to *The Henry Miller Reader* that Miller was "at peace with his neighbor, reconciled to friend and foe alike," Henry, furious, replied that he was never reconciled to America. Whenever I saw Henry, whether in Paris or in California, I was always struck by his rancor for his country, and rather than mellowing with the passage of the years, it had only seemed to grow more virulent.

Homesickness wasn't the only thing pulling him back to the States. There was also an urgent, imperious need to hear native English. For five years he had had almost no access to the latest street slang; it was to fill his ears with the British version of it that he had undertaken that ill-fated trip to Newhaven three years earlier. Inspired by Céline, Miller viewed written language as an alliance between the literary and the spoken. Before Paris, he had thought the word *written* carried far more weight than the word *spoken*, but he had changed his mind; not only was the language of ordinary people, with all its neologisms and ellipses, more direct, more spontaneous, more alive, but it was also more muscular and durable than "literary" language. Henry wanted to reinvigorate and enrich his vocabulary — all the more urgent given that the books he was working on were set in the United States and New York — by plunging back into the streets and merging with the crowd. He also wanted to revisit some of the streets and neighborhoods of his past, to go to Brooklyn, Broadway, and Greenwich Village. When he got to New York, he even took a room in the same neighborhood in which he had worked at his father's tailor shop.

Anaïs joined him in New York, and for her it was a strange and moving experience to see all the places Henry had talked and written about. He took her to the vacant lots, the sheet-metal factory he describes in *Black Spring*, the row-housed streets of his first dreams and disappointments. Henry also showed her the basement apartment he had shared with June. It had been turned into a Chinese restaurant.

Still another reason for the return to New York was to make contact with those literary magazines that might be interested in publishing one of his works. Henry had convinced himself that approaching book editors was a waste of time, given that unless he agreed to mutilate them by excising the obscene passages, his books would remain unpublishable in the United States. Among the few works that might have been suitable for magazine format was "The Eye of Paris," and Henry bombarded me with letters urging me to send photographs of Parisian slums to illustrate it. "Dear Brassaï," he wrote in February 1935, "I have just seen an editor at *Vanity Fair*. They say your work is well known. They've asked for a dozen or more of your photos — they might publish them — understood? With a small article by me. They don't want anything big." Eventually the article appeared in *The Globe*, out of Chicago, in November 1937, taking up eight pages plus the cover. The article consisted of several fragments of "The Eye of Paris," including the following:

What a procession passes before my eyes! What a throng of men and women! What strange cities — and situations stranger still! The mendicant sitting on the public bench, thirsting for a glimmer of sun, the butcher standing in a pool of blood with knife upraised, the scows and barges dreaming in the shadows of the bridges, the pimp standing against a wall with cigarette in hand, the street cleaner with her broom of reddish twigs, her thick, gnarled fingers, her high stomach draped in black, a shroud over her womb, rinsing away the vomit of the night before so that when I pass over the cobblestones my feet will gleam with the light of morning stars.

This somewhat slight piece was the sole fruit of Miller's "American campaign," which lasted longer than he had thought it would: five months in all, from December 1934 to May 1935. Miller later wrote that he was satisfied with the trip: now twelve men and one woman in New York knew he was a "genius."

XVII

Anaïs Drifts Away

Things between Anaïs and Henry started to unravel in the spring of 1936. Their irresolvable differences had begun to take their toll, and that great friendship, so liberating for Anaïs and so nurturing for Henry, began to lose steam. Anaïs acknowledged this, though not without some bitterness: "The differences separating Henry and myself are becoming more marked. Differences in personality, habit, books, and even differences with regard to writing itself" (*Diary*, vol. 2). She was very disillusioned. After the joyful novelty of slumming around with Henry in Montmartre and Montparnasse, diving into the low-life shallows of Paris, Anaïs had in the end grown weary of bohemian life. She had never liked crowds, and spending long hours in packed cafés or roaming aimlessly through Paris streets until dawn had almost become torture. Henry might be able to spend hours and hours in smoky bars, engaging in meaningless banter with Fraenkel and other friends, or loitering in disreputable streets with the down-and-out, but she was fed up with it.

She was not at all charmed by the atmosphere at the Villa Seurat, "with its schoolboy pranks, clownish humor, and taste for the burlesque." Her ordered and logical sensibility was increasingly bruised by Henry's impulsive recklessness. All those side tracks and detours. She began criticizing him for the way he would make fun of an idea the very minute he had expressed it, and for pushing everything to the point of parody: sex, ideas, life. Laughing, Miller defended himself by saying that burlesque was the best form of destruction, but Anaïs, who sought desperately to find some certainties in life, some tangible values, thought that one could not always be destructive about everything. She wanted Henry to commit himself to some idea, to say yes or no to it. Man must show character, loyalty, and responsibility, as Henry himself believed. A man of contradictions, Miller also embraced absurdity, the irrational, even chaos.

Fed by Perlès's clowning and by Durrell's off-color jokes, the freewheeling buffoonery of the Villa Seurat found its ultimate expression in *The Booster*, a small magazine, originally belonging to the American Country Club, that Fred, acting as "editor in chief," had transformed into a literary magazine. Here was the Villa Seurat's official vehicle! (All of the contributors — with the exception of Hilaire Hilaire and William Saroyan — lived there). Perlès had the time of his life appointing "Charles Norden" (Lawrence Durrell) as sports commentator, Anaïs as social columnist, and, of all things, Miller as fashion editor! After all, hadn't Stéphane Mallarmé edited a fashion magazine? Perlès, Miller, and Durrell teamed up to write a "Special Letter to Celebrities." Three editions of *The Booster* managed to make their way into print, and the magazine survived for a couple more under the name *Delta*. This was the last straw for Anaïs. She found the magazine vulgar and grotesque, and was convinced Henry was wasting his energies on it, energies better spent writing novels. Later he would admit she had been right.

Anaïs had also had it with Miller's cynicism, with what she saw as his lack of human feeling. The Spanish Civil War, hunger, fear, misery, bombings — nothing seemed to touch him. To this "happy rock," as he cheerfully referred to himself, the world could do whatever it wished so long as he could still use his typewriter. Anaïs began to feel that Miller was anesthetized to the world, incapable of deeper attachment and affairs of the heart. The deeper sources of feeling had evaporated, as had also happened to Joaquin Nin, Anaïs's father, whom she described as a "distant, drifting, lifeless iceberg."

There is truth to what she says. We might keep in mind that Miller descended in a direct line from Emersonian transcendentalism, from a mystical pantheism and a pantheistic mysticism whose primary function was to help an individual discover his own particular fate and to find a balance with the cosmos. Miller preached that the best way to help the world was to be the only one of one's kind. Within the realm of this egocentric philosophy, all that really counts is the inner world — the relationship between man and the immensity of the universe. To social problems it is blind and deaf. Henry was only concerned with social problems in his very early youth. "Today," he writes in the final *Hamlet* letter, "I believe that it is possible to be in the world and of it and at the same time beyond it, an attitude which was impossible for me at the age of twenty-one because I did not know the world, because at that time I was intent on *altering* the world, and that in the most ineffective way possible, by a straight-lined, idealistic attitude."

Anaïs felt this same absence of emotion in *Tropic of Capricorn*, of which she had read several passages in manuscript. She didn't care about the obscenity, but she was disturbed by the remorseless obsession with sex and by what she saw as its dessicating absence of romance. Miller's great universe was ultimately dominated by depersonalized, anonymous sex. "Instead of investing each woman with a different face," Anaïs wrote him in March 1937, "you take pleasure in reducing all women to an aperture, to a biological sameness." Prefiguring feminism, Anaïs thought Miller's depictions of women were purely exploitative. "Your depersonalization is leading you so far, you are disintegrating so much that it all becomes sex, and sex is a hole, and after that death. Oblivion." She tells Henry that the only woman to have emerged from the sea of women in Henry's work with any individuality was June, and this was because she had known how to torture him. Anaïs had already noted in her *Diary* that she could no longer take part in life at the Villa Seurat: "I need to create my own universe." Not long after she'd written this, a new passion came into her life.

★　　　★　　　★

One evening my friend the painter and photographer Emile Savitry took me to the basement apartment of one of his Peruvian friends, not far from the Lion de Belford on Rue Boulard. Managing to make my way down a series of unlit steps, I found myself in a cave straight out of one of Maxim Gorky's "nether regions." It was a dark labyrinth with crumbling walls that looked as if they'd once been destroyed in a fire, and lit only by oil lamps. The gas and electricity had apparently been long since cut off.

Shadowy forms began emerging from the darkness, and finally I was able to make out a young woman standing at an easel, painting. This was Elsa, the Peruvian with whom Emile was in love and whom he would later marry.

Against her pale face, wan from living in the cave, her large, dark eyes looked as if they were on fire. Her dark hair fell all the way to the small of her back and was knotted with a piece of red taffeta. From another room I could hear the sounds of a violin. A moment later a skeletal figure emerged. He was the double of Paganini. His expansive bald skull and gigantic black eyes made him look like a corpse in a *danse macabre*. A real skeleton was hanging from a perch in the cave — a learning tool, as it turned out, for a young Peruvian medical student. Suddenly there was a tremendous noise, like someone firing an automatic rifle. Her black hair flying, the dancer Helba Huara started to perform an Incan dance. Her heels hammered madly against the steps, which, for lack of floor space, she had to move up and down, her castanets all the while engaged in furious dialogue. The atmosphere was like the one in the wildly successful 1930s film *You Can't Take it With You*, but less wacky and more authentic. Then a man with noble bearing appeared. It was Gonzalo. I had seen him in Montparnasse without realizing that he was Helba Huara's husband. He would have been hard to miss. He was a head taller than anyone else, his almond-shaped eyes were carbon black and framed by incredibly long eyelashes, and he had a high forehead over which tumbled black, unkempt hair already streaked with white. His skin was black. Other friends arrived: a young, birdlike blond woman with eyes like forget-me-nots who was descended from one of Russia's great families, escorted by a young Adonis (who was apparently as much of an anarchist as she). Gonzalo built up the fire, on which a paella, made by Emile, was slowly cooking. At about 11:00 P.M., famished, we finally gathered around a long kitchen table covered with red wine stains and wax from melted candles. We were about to eat when a band of starved Peruvians descended into the smoky cave like a cloud of locusts, and everyone's portion of paella instantly got smaller.

★　　　★　　　★

Anaïs had already attended a Peruvian dance recital at a small theater on Rue de la Gaîté that featured an assortment of strange and very wild dances with names like "The Woman Without Arms" and "The Woman Transformed into a Puma." They were inspired by a combination of voodoo, Incan legends, and Indian poetry, and left a profound impression on her. Helba appeared, immobile, dressed in some extraordinary costume of her own design made out of napkins, breadbaskets, brooms — whatever was at hand. The greatest admirer of these nightmarish performances was Antonin Artaud. He was passionate about Indian mythology and had sought out Gonzalo's help in writing an essay on the subject. Henry had also met Gonzalo at a reception. Anaïs reports that they got drunk and got along famously, convinced as they both were that any sort of work was a crime.

Roger Klein then told Anaïs the whole romantic story of the two Peruvians. Gonzalo had been a theater-and-dance critic for a big newspaper in Lima, and that was how he had met Helba, who was dancing in a nightclub. Promised in marriage at the age of fourteen, she was miserable. Gonzalo fell in love with her, and they ran off together to New York. He was disowned by his family and they struggled to survive. By a stroke of luck, Helba was hired to appear in a Ziegfeld show. Things seemed about to improve when suddenly there was more drama. Very suddenly, Helba went completely deaf and had to quit the stage. They decided to move to France, where Helba continued to give dance performances, though only to a small circle of acquaintances and without earning a living at it. Their pitiable state aroused Anaïs's sympathies and she decided she wanted to meet them. The memorable meeting took place in Roger's studio apartment on Rue des Artistes. Gonzalo played guitar and sang Peruvian songs. He asked Anaïs to dance. It was love at first sight for both of them. Gonzalo became obsessed with one idea and one idea alone: to see this fragile, airy creature again, this "Renaissance virgin" so animated by sensitivity and intelligence. He told her she was the perfume and the essence of all things. Anaïs, for her part, was enthralled by the dark beauty of this Incan, with his nobility, his mystery, his spontaneity and human warmth — by his romanticism, in short. She was a little afraid where things might go with this "tiger without claws," but by that point it was already too late for second thoughts.

She sold her house in Louveciennes, and in a light, brand-new apartment on the Quai de Passy — far from Montparnasse — with windows that opened onto the sparkling Seine, she gave a "tropical night" party in honor of her new Peruvian friends. A group of Tahitian dancers and singers performed. Gonzalo fascinated Anaïs all the more by speaking in Spanish, a language she had not spoken since the age of six, and in which words "came as if through the underground channel of ancestral memory" — words that engaged not her mind but her body and her blood, words that awoke sensual reactions of the sort Anaïs had not before known. Through this passion she rediscovered the world of her ancestry, everything she had inherited from ardent and mystical Spain.

Gonzalo had been a pampered child of a rich and powerful Peruvian family, and had grown up in a large hacienda with a staff of nearly a hundred Indians. But in Paris he became an anarchist. He waited for the revolution, the uprising of the Indians in South America. When civil war broke out in Spain, he wanted to sign up to help the Republicans, and was ready to give his all for the great cause. He didn't, in the end. Instead he gave himself over to bourgeois virtues — though also to culture, art, intellectuals, and artists, everything so dear to the heart of Anaïs. Even though she was far from convinced of the necessity or use of revolution, Anaïs, out of curiosity and love, allowed herself to get dragged into the very heart of Marxist politics. Thus did this worldly woman, the embodiment of elegance and luxury, take off her jewelry, change out of her high-fashion dresses, and let her hair down, so that she could go to political meetings sometimes attended by Gide and Malraux. Soon her name was inscribed on the list of partisans for a republican Spain. She even bought a printing press so that Gonzalo could publish his revolutionary tracts.

Not long after, one of Anaïs's greatest dreams came true: to live on a houseboat on the Seine. Michel Simon, an actor and friend of Henry's, had lived on the *Belle Aurore* for quite some time, but the chimpanzees he had living with him had attacked some passersby and he was forced to abandon ship. On this houseboat, secret meetings of Latin American revolutionaries were held. Like autumn mists, they would roll in, ready to compose propaganda literature and recite the poems of Neruda and Alberti. For Anaïs, however, disillusionment soon followed. Living with Gonzalo meant confronting his contradictions — he was both anticlerical and religious, Marxist and mystic, an enemy to the arts and passionate about painting. His romanticism and Incan nonchalance hid a lazy streak, and his rebelliousness was erratic. The hard-bitten anarchist was really only playacting, and in the end he turned out to be a smooth talker who couldn't live up to his promises and would forget his commitments.

XVIII

Larry Arrives

Many of those who would go on to become Henry's closest friends began their friendship by reading *Tropic of Cancer*, and being electrified by it. Twenty-three-year-old Lawrence Durrell was on the Island of Corfu when he was jolted by Henry's messy and unnerving book, a book that defied all the canons of good taste and literary convention. He immediately sat down to write Miller a letter, which Miller, when he received it, knew immediately was not written by an average reader — but by someone with vitality and gifts, someone who could himself write beautifully. What was to make "Larry" all the more fascinating and appealing in Henry's eyes was that he had been born in northern India, near Tibet, at the foot of the Himalayas, a region of the world that for his entire life Henry would regard as a sort of promised land. He was moved to tears when he read Larry's description of his childhood in a letter of January 1937: "Until eleven marvelous memories — white, white the Himalayas from the dormitory windows. The gentle black

Jesuits praying to our lady and outside on the frontier roads the Chinese walking stiffly and Tibetans playing cards on the ground: the blue fissures in the hills." Henry was persuaded that by having looked upon the lushest landscapes and the whitest mountaintops the world had to offer, his young friend had absorbed all the magic and mystery of India.

After an exchange of letters that became increasingly friendly, Durrell, accompanied by his wife, Nancy, whom he had married a year earlier, arrived in Paris in September 1937 and descended upon the Villa Seurat. He was a robust, young Englishman of twenty-six with blue eyes and astonishing self-assurance. He had a poet's tongue and sparkling laughter, and was bursting with life. Miller recalled that Larry's arrival among them caused a sensation: fresh from the sunny Mediterranean and dying to immerse himself in "decadent Paris." Under the influence of *Tropic of Cancer*, which he believed the greatest book of the century, Durrell had written *The Black Book*, which, with Miller's assistance, was published by the Obelisk Press. He arrived in Paris just at the moment when the Popular Front[1] was feverishly preparing its International Exposition at the foot of the Eiffel Tower. One morning, Durrell left Henry a note that shows the playful wit he brought to the Villa Seurat: "1. What do you do with the garbage and 2. When you say 'to be with God' do you identify yourself with God: or do you regard the God-stuff reality as something *extraneous* towards which we yearn?" For six months, Fred, Larry, and Henry —

---

[1] Translator's note: The Popular Front, whose full title was the Popular Front for Defense against Fascism, had been founded to counteract a growing rightist movement in France in the early 1930s. Under Léon Blum's leadership, it had won in the 1936 elections. A Spanish pavilion at the World's Fair in Paris opened its doors in July 1937. The Popular Front organized demonstrations to show its support for the Republicans in the Spanish Civil War, which had been going on for a year.

"The Three Musketeers," as they called themselves — had the time of their lives.

There were some subjects that weren't to be taken lightly. For example, Miller made it clear that he thought it unacceptable that, after *The Black Book* had been published, that his young friend should continue to write under the pseudonym "Van Norden": "You can't look two ways," he wrote him in July 1937. "You've got to accept the responsibility for your actions." Durrell defended himself by saying that what looked like self-compromise was actually self-defense. Using a pseudonym was indispensable if he was to write things he didn't take all that seriously. But Henry wouldn't be budged on the subject: "You can't be alone and be with the herd too. You can't write good *and* bad books. Not for long . . . The toll is 'disintegration.'" Yet Henry himself had given Larry an example of someone who did just that — Balzac. Balzac's early works, written during a drunken youth, were starter novels. It wasn't until *The Last Chan* appeared that the true, the serious Balzac was to surface. Henry somehow couldn't accept the idea that Larry might be following Balzac's example, sharpening his skills and familiarizing himself with different writing styles and angles of vision before becoming the author of *The Alexandria Quartet*. Durrell went on writing journalist pieces, telling his friend that he needed to do it to "pay for baby's shoes." Miller replied by saying that baby would be happier without shoes. Durrell stuck to his guns — and found that his short pieces did more than pay for baby's shoes. "I am in the process of learning to write by a process [of] progressive unselfimportance and my experience of *forms* is paying off," he wrote Miller. "I can write in several different modes without straining by suddenly realising how unimportant it is to write at all!"

For his part, Durrell, who was himself a careful stylist,

grew to become critical of Miller's excesses. In September 1948, he wrote Henry that he thought that half of *Murder the Murderer* could have been "blue-penciled out." He found it "repetitive and platitudinous." "Like all American geniuses you have no sense of form whatsoever," he teased him.

A more serious issue nearly broke up their friendship. Anaïs had always insisted that a process of "spiritualization" would take place in Henry's work, that eventually the mind would triumph. "In *Tropic of Cancer*," she wrote in her *Diary*, "you are nothing but a penis and a stomach. In *Black Spring*, you start to have eyes, a heart, ears, hands. With each book you will gradually turn into a complete man" (*Diary*, vol. 2). In his youthful impatience, Durrell couldn't stop thinking about the books Henry was to write, and even sketched out some lines they might take. He bathed Miller in celestial light, and believed fervently, as he writes in January 1937, that Miller would be the one writer to produce the work that "will bust open the void."

Durrell expected nothing less than a new *Faust* or *Hamlet*, a "Hamlet *squared*, Hamlet *cubed:* Hamlet in an atmosphere which gives trigonometry cold fingers, and logic blunt thumbs." In nearly Mephistophelean fashion, he continues to tempt Miller in his letters: "You are looking round and beginning to see the shapes of things. That ultimate battle, which I tremble when I think about, is almost announced. IN ALL THAT IS YOU WILL BE SUBJECTED TO THE DRAMA. YOU WILL LOOSE YOUR POWER OVER THE ARMIES, and the result will be those immense mythical figures which will fertilise all our books for centuries and our minds. I tell you this in confidence." Miller was so hypnotized by the new direction that his close friends seemed to expect of him that he got taken in. "Oddly enough," he wrote Durrell back, "I too have felt that the great opus lies ahead, and in somewhat the manner indicated. Not *Capricorn*, which will be tremendous enough, I can assure you. No, something of a wholly different order. Something to put beside *Quixote, Gargantua, Satyricon,* etc. A classic for the 21st or 22nd century."[2]

Instead of the great book that would "bust open the void," Durrell got *Sexus*. He was horrified, and immediately sent Henry a telegram saying that the book was a disaster and should be destroyed immediately. A letter, dated September 5, 1949, followed: "What a pity, what a terrible pity for a major artist not to have critical sense enough to husband his forces, to keep his talent aimed at the target." Most of all, he reproaches Henry for not having developed the element of mysticism that would have brought him new laurels: "[Y]ou have failed to develop what is really new in your prose, and what should set a crown on your work — the new mystical outlines are all there; but they are lost, lost damn it in this shower of lavatory filth which no longer seems tonic and bracing, but just excrementitious and sad."

The vehemence of Durrell's reaction would have been enough to "bust open" most friendships, and it was a testament to the largeness of Henry's spirit that he bore his friend no grudge. He had learned from Whitman to accept even the most acerbic criticism without bitterness. "You don't suppose that after all I've been through," he wrote Larry in October 1949, "I would fold up because a dear friend happened not to like what I wrote, do you?" Though he had long since stopped defending his work to critics, he felt he should try to explain himself to Larry: "I am trying to reproduce in words a block of my life which to me has the utmost significance — every bit

---

[2] Even after the war, lots of Miller's disciples thought that he would evolve toward spirituality. The minister J. P. Hornus already discerned what he thought was a conversion away from a "material Eros" to a "spiritual Eros," from lust for the flesh to lust for the spirit. But Henry immediately discouraged Hornus from presuming that there was a "moral" turn to his evolution. — *Au.*

of it . . . Since 1927 I have carried inside me the material of this book. Do you suppose it's possible that I could have a miscarriage after such a period of gestation? . . . But Larry, I can never go back on what I've written. If it was not good, it was true; if it was not artistic, it was sincere; if it was in bad taste, it was on the side of life." If there was one word that Miller found hard to forgive, it was "vulgarity." "Sometimes I think that you, Larry, never really knew what it was to live in our modern age — of asphalt and chemicals. To grow up in the street, to speak the language of the Voyou."

Ten years later, when Durrell undertook to write an introduction to an anthology of Miller's work, Henry made him this proposition: "[Y]ou could say all those things I think you ought and want to say — about my weaknesses, my limitations, my bad writing, my obsessions, my lack of self-criticism, etc. etc. etc. I've had plenty of laudatory comments and lots of picayune criticism from little shits, but you could really blast me — it would be fun."

Miller reproached Durrell for writing for money; Larry disapproved of the way Miller allowed his work to be published without getting an honest cut. If he behaved like an "established" writer, if he wrote pieces for the "established" magazines, in three years, Durrell was convinced, Miller would be considered the greatest living American writer. "*I* can't take measures to preserve my reputation," Miller wrote him in October 1951, "Me and my reputation will always be separate things."

The truth is that Miller wrote "for lack of something better" and refused to become the great man of letters Durrell wanted him to be. For his part, Durrell wanted to master form, to chisel literature into a state of perfection. Miller saw writing as a way of finding Goethe's "life's traces." He wanted to express himself completely; Durrell wanted him to depersonalize himself. Durrell bemoans

Miller's "poor literary sense"; Miller reproaches his young friend for assuming the "makers of literature" are the "masters of art." "Where does creation lie — in the thing done or in the effect? What and how a man does, acts, thinks, talks, every day is what counts, no?" Miller teased Durrell for his precociousness, but also called him the greatest writer in England. After he'd read *Justine*, he told Durrell that "nobody can wield the English language like you. Hair-raising sometimes." "One can see how you have struggled to master the medium, and not just the medium, but the language itself, the English, the King's English. Now I read you enviously."

The man who boasted that he had always remained a Brooklyn kid and spoke the language of the "voyou" while making fun of pretty writing can't find words strong enough in "the King's English" to praise Durrell. "There's no one alive writing like this," he wrote in November 1958 after reading *Mountolive*. "You're king now."

Miller envied more than just Durrell's mastery of language; he envied his reserve. "When I think of all you have endured these past fifteen years or more and of how discreetly, tactfully silent you have been, I grow ashamed of myself." The man who had thought that the self was the key to his work praised Durrell for having "kept all this nasty personal dreck" out of his books. Miller's whole lifework was this "personal dreck." Durrell did not fall for this self-deprecation. He saw very clearly the gulf between talent, brilliant though it might be, and true genius. For all Miller's platitudes and repetitions, a "Herculean genius" is what Durrell always knew him to be.

XIX

The Astrological Henry Miller

Anaïs thought he wasn't the same man at all. This was not the cynical, vengeful, "dried-up" Henry Miller she had known, the one who only knew how to "spit and lie in the gutters of *Tropic of Cancer*" — but a creator, a poet who'd given himself over to meditation, reading, and introspection, who'd renounced the ways of the world and become luminous with the tolerance, acceptance, and wisdom of the Chinese. In his later Paris years, Henry went through a mystical period. The metaphysical tendencies slumbering within him since childhood very suddenly awoke and made him alive to the teachings of Swedenborg, Meister Eckhardt, and Jacob Boehme, all of whom, thanks to R. H. Hamilton, he had known in his youth. Madame Blavatsky's *Secret Doctrine* and *Isis Unveiled* had also had a profound influence on him very early on. Like Whitman, Miller detested religious creeds and railed against preachers, but he was attracted by the founders of the great religions. He had dreams himself of being a shaman, a guru, a magician, a magus, and regretted not having known the Holy Russia of the nineteenth century, with its novelists, revolutionaries, and visionaries. He also regretted not having been born on Christmas; his "lazy" mother had held him in her womb one day too many.

Such words as *esoteric, mystic, occult,* and *alchemy* could make Miller's soul vibrate. "Every time I pick up a mystical book I am struck again, shuttled back, as it were, to some fundamental truthful realm of my self which has been so much denied in life," he wrote to Durrell in January 1939. The occult expressed life's darker sides and mysterious dimensions, and Miller always said he felt pulled between the poles of the erotic and the esoteric, like the lotus flower caught between earth and heaven, putting down its roots at the river's edge.

★   ★   ★

Among those of Miller's friends who frequented the Zeyer Café was a secretive, anxious-looking man who almost never laughed. His name was David Edgar. An American who had arrived in Paris at the same time as Henry, Edgar was steeped in mysticism, and initiated Henry into the ways of the occult: the theosophy of Annie Besant, E. Graham Low, and Rudolph Steiner, and especially Chinese and Hindu doctrines. Henry read Confucius, Lao-tsu, and Tay Young-Ming, marveling at their reserve and admiring their condemnation of illusion. Through Edgar, Henry was introduced to yoga and, more important, to Zen Buddhism, the philosophy he found closest to his heart and his temperament. "All these great birds of Tibet remind me of the Zen masters," he wrote to Durrell in 1939, "who are up my street. Zen is my idea of life absolutely — the closest thing to what I am unable to formulate in words. I am a Zen addict through and through . . . No intelligent person, no sensitive person, can help but be a Buddhist. It's clear as a bell to me." "You know," he'd written Durrell three years earlier, "I'm nuts about China. I always think that that is the place I will eventually wind up in. I *feel* like a Chinaman very often." Among the living Hindu wisemen, Krishnamurti was the only one whose influence Miller felt no hesitation about acknowledging. Rather than as a "prophet," Henry saw him as a human being whose single desire was to restore dignity to life. Krishnamurti lived in Ojai, California, little more than a hundred miles from Big Sur, and although Miller hoped someday to meet him, this never happened.

★   ★   ★

Miller's passion for astrology dates from about this same time. His first master was Eduardo Sánchez, one of Anaïs's cousins. After Sánchez he consulted with a number of other magi, notably with Walter Freeman, who had predicted that Henry was just beginning a "splendid" artistic cycle. But if astrology became a central part of Miller's life, it was most of all because of Conrad Moricand.

Moricand had been among the guests at Anaïs's houseboat-warming party in the summer of 1936. A friend of Blaise Cendrars and Max Jacobs — with whom he had collaborated on *The Mirror of Astrology* [*Le Miroir de l'Astrologie*] — Moricand had done horoscopes for Modigliani, Cocteau, Mac Orlan, and Picasso. This pale and aristocratic creature, born to wealthy Swiss parents, used his Parisian studio as a salon, giving dinner parties and devoting himself to his passion for the occult. After the death of his parents, Moricand was suddenly on his own. He decided that he would live the only way he knew how — by casting horoscopes. Anaïs recommended him to all her friends and, in the fall of 1936, to Miller, who embraced him all the more warmly when he learned that he and Moricand were both Capricorns (though they were not, he noted, of the same decan). When I met him, Moricand was living in a tiny hotel room on Rue Notre-Dame-De-Lorette, and though he had fallen far from the sumptuous days of yore, he kept up appearances. His dandyish apparel had already gone out of fashion by the mid-thirties, the days of the Popular Front — it even looked a little ridiculous — yet he always wore starched cuffs and collars, gaiters, and yellow gloves, and still doused himself with eau de cologne. His bearing stiff, his shoes polished to a gloss, his trouser creases sharp, Moricand didn't look in the slightest as you'd imagine an astrologer to look. Indeed, by the time I met him, requests for his horoscopes had been declining steadily. If it hadn't been for Anaïs, he might have starved to death. Miller later wondered if Anaïs hadn't recommended Moricand to him as a way of getting him off her back, but he did everything he could to help out, encouraging his friends to have Moricand cast their horoscopes (at the reasonable price of fifty francs, the price of two or three dinners). Henry truly admired this singular-looking man's impressive gifts. Moricand could immediately deduce anyone's zodiacal sign, and never made a mistake. He was clairvoyant. I remember that after doing Hitler's chart he said that all the signs pointed to his "dying very soon — perhaps assassinated."

Naturally, Henry was most interested in his own chart, which I remember seeing written out in chalk on one of the walls at the Villa Seurat. It was the source of violent debates between Miller and Moricand. Miller was preoccupied with the details of his birth, which had taken place at noon on December 26, 1891 — a Saturday — on East

Eighty-fifth Street in Manhattan. The conjunction of the moon, which was in the Eighth House, with Uranus, the rebel, in the Seventh House, and with Mars, the fighter, all indicated a great capacity for work, courage, energy, a taste for risk. But it also predicted there would be conflict with those around him, and serious conjugal difficulties; indeed, it predicted that there would be many separations. And there were. What interested Henry particularly about his chart was Uranus's conjunction with Venus. According to Moricand, the conjunction explained Miller's original way of representing sexuality. Saturn's dissonant aspect was a source of worry to Henry. If he felt depressed or even suicidal, he attributed it to Saturn's nefarious influence. His letters of the time contain quite a few allusions to the position of the stars and its effect on his current mood. Moricand tried to reassure Miller about Saturn. The planet's evil aspect, he said, was more than compensated for by Jupiter's friendly, harmonious, and protective aspects. Jupiter would help him achieve ease, riches, and fame. Miller drank these words in greedily. One night, after a talk with the astrologer, he decided he wanted to get a better look at his lucky planet, so, using a metal ladder, he climbed up to the flat roof of the Villa Seurat. He was so absorbed by the sight that he tripped and tumbled off the roof, falling with a huge crash through a window. Covered in cuts and bleeding profusely, Henry thought his life was over. Happily, his neighbor, Arno de Maitret, came to his rescue and took him to the American Hospital in Neuilly, where he was stitched up.

Did this mean he should abandon astrology altogether? Not in the slightest. When Moricand heard what had happened — so Henry tells us — he ran to Miller's bedside, brandishing his horoscope. He told Miller that in fact he'd been incredibly lucky. The astral conjunctions had been stacked against Henry, and it was thanks to Jupiter that he'd survived the fall, because Jupiter had been the only planet in his horoscope not in a bad aspect on that particular evening.

In 1947, Moricand sent Miller a cry for help from Switzerland. Broken physically and financially, he asked Miller to invite him to Big Sur. Henry obligingly sent him the travel money. He soon realized what a parasite Moricand was. The whole tragicomic story of Moricand's stay in Big Sur is the subject of Miller's *A Devil in Paradise*.

Moricand was not Miller's only astrologer. Before and after him, there had been and would be others. In 1933, of course, Freeman had predicted the beginning of Henry's "splendid cycle"; there was the astrologer Henry went to visit at the Crystal Palace in London; there was another he consulted in Périgueux. In California he became an admirer of the famous Rudhyar. One young man, whom he calls "Claude" in *Plexus*, and who Miller believed had the gift of prophecy, predicts that Henry is about to leave on a long trip. He advises Miller to sweep away all the doubts plaguing him: "A being like yourself has only to throw himself on the world and he will float like a cork. Nothing truly evil will ever touch you or affect you. You were made to walk though the fires." Every astrologer Henry consulted predicted that things were looking up for him, and for a dozen or so years, Miller devoted himself to astrology and listened to its oracles. When he learned that Whitman had been born under Gemini, he felt he understood him better. He always believed that Goethe was the finest example of a Virgo who ever lived. He was sure that reproducing a writer's horoscope in his book would greatly facilitate a reader's understanding of both. Knowing Spengler's horoscope would have given him a key to understanding the character of the author of *The Decline of the West*. Miller was always upset when he learned that an astrologer whom he just then considered a true prophet was suspected of being a rip-off artist, though his own repudiation of astrology, when it happened, was sudden and total. Nonetheless, all his life, Miller believed in a lucky star, and was convinced that a powerful presence watched over his life.

XX

Farewell to France

Miller went through a very difficult time on the eve of the war. The windfall he had been waiting for hadn't come. The world was still greeting his work with reticence. The rejections from French publishers, the sloppiness of the Obelisk Press, the banning of his books in America — these were all discouraging. He wondered if he was writing in a void. The plentiful press clippings on *Tropic of Cancer* and *Black Spring* provided clear proof that he was becoming a known figure, even a celebrity, but he still felt as if he were spinning his wheels. Yet, always the impenitent optimist, he also continued to believe in his star, and continued to refuse to compromise his work for the sake of getting into print. Frank Dobo had been sending Henry's manuscripts around to several American publishing houses. He was told that if the obscenities were expunged from Miller's works, they would be published. Frank told me that at the moment he had passed this news along to Henry, the latter was completely broke. The royalties alone must have seemed like a fortune to him.

But he wouldn't back down. It was an act of heroism on Henry's part. When he wrote his letter refusing the publishers' offer, he didn't even have the money to put a stamp on it, and had to ask Frank to send it for him.

On March 1939, two months before he left Paris, Miller wrote to Frank from the Brasserie Zeyer and told him that he was in desperate need of money:

Dear Dobo,

I just sent off my fifth book, written out by hand and illustrated in my way, to Emil Schnellock in Orange, Vaucluse. Each manuscript is a one-of-its-kind. There are no copies. Written specially for the person to whom it was sent. And up to now, *gratuit.*

I was thinking today what a shame it is that I can't earn a little money for my labors of love. Someone in America, realizing that someday my work will become famous, should ask me to do a book like it — *pour de l'argent.* I would do anything for 100 dollars paid in cash in advance. In a few years, the book would be worth a thousand dollars, and in a century it would be invaluable. It would be put in a glass case in a museum or in the Bibliothèque Nationale.

Maintenant, I need money! *Alors,* find me a client. Naturally I would insist on absolute freedom. The buyer can tell me the subject he's chosen. It's all the same to me. I can write on anything — for a hundred dollars. I use the covers at the printer's for that. I choose a format that I like. You follow?

So my dear Dobo think about it long and tenderly. Realize that I am getting nothing from my rights because my debts swallow everything. I live from day to day. What I spend on stamps would keep a fox terrier in luxury. I have no vices and few pleasures. I lead *une vie solitaire* and only think of my "next" book. I have four books ready for publication and my publisher tells me to hold off — *il veut les espacer, les espacer, expèce de con, qu'il est! Et moi, je mourrai de faim! Alors, faites quelque chose. Pour un ami, je ferai un prix réduit. Mais il faut* — cash d'advance!

La vie est belle, quand on peut manger, sortir, danser, faire l'amour. Et caetera [sic]! *Je ne demande pas mieux que de vivre. Je n'aime pas être l'esclave-écrivain — une putain de vie, ça! J'adore le luxe, le soleil, le loisir, la vie oisive, quoi! Je fais des aquarelles entre-temps, mais ça ne me rapporete rien non plus! Je suis maudit* — *apprécié par les Suédois et les Tchèques et c'est tout. Je n'aime pas les éditeurs français* — *ils sont des salopards. Je les emmerde, tous!*

Quand viendra le jour où je peux sortir de ma prison? Etre libre, so promener comme les autres? Je ne veux pas une auto, ni un chien — *mais l'argent de poche, et c'est tout.* [1] How are you, old top?

P.S. If you want to see the book, Henry Miller, which I just sent to Emil, go to Orange, Vaucluse, and ask for the property of Mr. L. B. Gray. He is there. He's got a whole library of my books. It's worth the trip.

By early 1938, Miller had few illusions about what was going to happen to Europe. Right at the moment when he

---

[1] Translator's note: This letter was written in English, except for the portion rendered here in French, of which a translation follows: "He wants me to space them out, bastard that he is. Meanwhile I will die from hunger. So do something, Dobo. For a friend I will offer reduced prices, but it will have to be cash in advance.

How sweet life is when you can eat, go out, dance, make love. Etcetera. All I ask for is means to live. I hate being a writer/slave — it's a whore's life. I adore luxury, the sun, leisure, the easy life. In the meantime I've been doing a few watercolors, but this won't bring me much of an income. I'm afraid I'm damned — appreciated only by the Swedes and the Czechs and no one else. French publishers are sons of bitches. Screw them all.

Will the day come when I can leave my prison? Take walks, like everyone else? I don't want a car or a dog — just pocket money."

thought he had become master of his fate, the world was spinning out of control. His peace, his security, his work — everything was being put in jeopardy. Even though he inhabited his own little universe at the Villa Seurat, a universe from which he banished politics and rumors of war, the heat from the growing conflagration was beginning to make itself felt. The result was confusion. One minute Miller had suddenly made up his mind to join the French Foreign Legion, the next his irrepressible antimilitarism would kick in and he found the very notion revolting. We might remember that Miller's grandfather had deserted from the German army during the War of 1870 [the Franco-Prussian War], and that that was why he'd been forced to emigrate to America. Henry had managed to avoid conscription in 1917 even though he was twenty-five. In the end, of course, Henry didn't enlist in the French Foreign Legion, and the result was that he felt guilty and relieved at the same time.

What impressed Miller was the fatalism with which the French seemed to be accepting the war. The mobilization of the army touched him deeply. He writes in *Hamlet:* "In the movies later, seeing a worker kissing his wife good-bye at the station — no drama, no sob stuff, no heroism, just grim acceptance, fate, fatality, French realism: that was like putting a spike through me." In "Vive la France," written in 1941, he wrote that the French were not a warlike people; they were without hate, and thought of war purely as a kind of civic duty. "But the uppermost thought in their minds, when discussing the subject, was the home-coming, the resumption of normal life, the return to their little niche, whatever it might happen to be. To me their attitude always seemed to reveal the highest form of courage: it was eminently pacifistic. They would fight out of a sense of duty and without hatred. That is why France is strong and why she will rise again and resume her place in the world." When life is considered the highest good, a reversal of values takes place: courage, patriotism and the spirit of sacrifice all seem idiotic; heroism turns into cowardice, disobedience and treason turn into sacred duties. To live, to survive, any and all means are justified.

To Céline, who had been a hero of World War I (he'd been decorated and had even appeared on the cover of *Petit Journal*), the fields of glory, sacrifice, and heroism came to seem to him, a quarter of a century later, little more than places of abomination. The chapters about the carnage of war in *Journey to the End of Night* are among the most phantasmagoric ever written. Staring at the eviscerated remains of his colonel, Bardamu says, "Too bad. If he hadn't taken off when the bullets first started to fly, he wouldn't have ended up like this." To the disillusioned Céline, war was nothing but "offal clotted with blood," "putrescent idiocy lacking in honor." "'Am I the only coward on the face of the earth?' I thought. And with what terror! . . . To be lost among two million crazy idiots armed to the teeth."

Miller thought heroism didn't mean marching straight ahead; it meant making a run for it. Desertion was an act of courage, and combat little more than an expression of the desire to rally around the "comforts of discipline," as he writes in "Murder the Murderer." "Those who want to fight should be allowed to do so," he adds. "But what I protest against, and what I will never admit to be right, is forcing a man against his will and his conscience to sacrifice his life for a cause which he does not believe in." He finds it a cause for shame that this same man should be considered an enemy to his country, and find himself in disgrace — even in prison — simply because he cannot bring himself to believe in the war. What one hears behind Miller's words, of course, is Thoreau, another American who revolted against society and indeed against the very idea of a "state." Miller shared Thoreau's dismissal of anything that limited a man's freedom and any power that disposed of him, against his will, as it saw fit. In its willingness to accede to the worst kind of aggression, Miller's unconditional pacifism now seems naive and quixotic, but in the thirties it found a powerful echo in the work of Jean Giono. Miller became Giono's friend and admirer not only because of his writings, but also because of the stand Giono took against the war, a stand that landed him in prison. "I would gladly give up this false name — that of France — that the most simple and the most humble of those who have died for it might live," Giono wrote in *Jean le Bleu*. "Nothing is worth the heart of a man . . . Life is needlessly squandered with the benediction of every church in a muddy, inglorious death. What sweet logic that is! . . . There is no glory in being French. There is but one glory: *in being alive!*" For Giono, neither fate nor the order of things could justify butchery.

Céline proposed an alliance with Hitler at any price. Miller's own words in the face of the Nazi threat seem no less "defeatist" in tone. If the Nazis occupied the Villa Seurat, despise and hate them though he might, he would submit to them, even polish their boots. To live, he would do anything for anyone. The best way to conquer Hitler was to surrender to him completely: "We forget that the conquerers are always conquered by the defeated. The surest way to defeat Hitler would, in my opinion, be for Europe to surrender willingly. I go further — I say let him have the whole world." What Miller forgot to add was that if the Roman Empire was any example, the victory of the vanquished might take centuries.

★   ★   ★

After the Munich agreement in 1938, Miller, appalled, wrote and telegraphed anyone who might be able to help him. He had no desire to die in an air raid. The man who so admired Oriental detachment was becoming agitated. Anaïs couldn't resist remarking that "Henry's Chinese wisdom hadn't been able to stand up to reality."

When he got three thousand francs from Kahane, Henry gave a hundred of it to Fred, a hundred to Moricand, and a hundred to Belmont — to be used for the next edition of *Volontés* — then left town. He went to Lourdes, where he hoped to find calm and regain his dignity. The countryside was beautiful, but he thought the town monstrous — especially that giant, illuminated crucifix on top of the mountain, which drove him crazy. Yet another looked down from over his bed in his hotel room. This was too much, and he ran from the whole "bloody Catholic farce." Twenty years later, Miller had dinner with the novelist Roger Grenier, who had grown up not far from Lourdes. The conversation turned to Henry's brief stay in Lourdes in 1938, and Miller told Grenier that he had taken the crucifix in his hotel room off the wall and then, not knowing where to put it, stuck it in the chamber pot.

After a short trip to Toulouse, Miller spent several anxious days in Bordeaux. It looked as if the German whip was not descending immediately, and he returned to Paris, though with the firm intention of giving up his apartment in the Villa Seurat. Durrell had long been urging Henry to come to Corfu, promising him a clean room with two windows on the sea and, as further enticement, his own bath. Henry had always turned him down before, feeling that working conditions at the Villa Seurat were optimal and that he shouldn't bestir himself. He also thought that no country would ever be as interesting as France. The war changed his mind. Miller decided to take Larry up on the invitation. He also took the money Larry had sent him for the trip. Greece would be his new port in the storm.

Henry gave away all of his possessions to friends, and

asked Anaïs to rescue the manuscripts that were still sitting in the safe at the Obelisk Press, and take them to the United States. These notes and manuscripts, he apparently wrote her, would be worth millions of dollars if he were to die. "Remember that I'm carrying a will with me and if I die I leave everything to you" (*Diary*, vol. 2).

Things began happening quickly. *Tropic of Capricorn* appeared on May 10, 1939, and two weeks later, on May 25, a Thursday, Miller left the Villa Seurat for good. While waiting for his visa for Greece, he spent several days in a small hotel near Montsouris Park, situated on a blind alley between Rue de l'Aude and Rue Saint-Yves. By June 10 he had reached Rocamadour, a place to which he was attracted purely because of the village's name. He visited the Gouffre de Padirac Cave, and had "a most memorable meal suspended between the bottom of the cave and the surface of the earth," as he recounts in "Vive la France." Then it was on to Dordogne. He found the Périgueux terribly dull. With its thirteenth- and fourteenth-century ramparts looking down on the river, the town of Dômme, on the other hand, enchanted him. This was the France that he had dreamed of, the real France. He then went to Sarlat, a town he'd never heard of before this trip, "on an impulse." Arriving in the evening, he took a stroll through the winding back streets and enjoyed the feeling of finding himself in the middle of the Middle Ages. A bookseller invited him to dinner, and gave him a copy of Nostradamus's prophecies. "My eyes were brimming with tears. The past was alive again; it lived in every façade, every portal, every cornice, in the very stones under our feet." He also went to the Eyzies Valley, with its prehistoric caves. He was deeply impressed by the cave drawings; he also said he'd eaten the best meal he'd ever had there, and that it had only cost him twenty francs.

Though he was growing weary of the succession

of towns and trains and hotel rooms, and of having to lug his suitcases around, Henry's boat for Piraeus didn't leave until the middle of July, so he visited places along the Côte d'Azur — Grasse, Cannes, Cagnes-sur-Mer, Nice, Monaco — and found himself wishing he'd lived in that part of the world. On July 14 he left Marseilles on the *Théophile Gautier*, bound for Greece. There was a brief stop in Naples, enough time to visit the city and Pompeii. On July 19, he arrived in Piraeus. He crossed the Peloponnese and joined Durrell in Corfu in August.

Henry left France without tears, without regret, and without looking back, as if the ten years he'd lived there had simply vanished. Behind him was a drab nightmare. Ahead, the sunny landscape of Greece. He was enthralled. He stopped reading books and didn't even bother glancing at what the kiosks were selling. Whether out of a deep need to purge himself of the past, or to deny the present, he completely ignored the world's suffering — the tragic fate that had befallen Poland and would soon be visited upon France — and reveled unapologetically in creature comforts: a drunken feast of sand, sea, and delicious food. He wrote in his diary that the world seemed well. Perhaps he needed the backdrop of a world caught up in fire and blood to enjoy the feelings of peace and contentment within himself all that much more intensely. "I never knew the meaning of peace until I arrived at Epidaurus," he wrote in *The Colossus of Maroussi*, which he thought the best book he had ever written. His stay in Greece provided him with his life's crowning moment. It was there that he could "start from scratch": "Other men are quicker to coordinate vision and action. But . . . in Greece I finally achieved that coordination. I became deflated, restored to proper human proportions, ready to accept my lot and prepared to give of all that I have received."

Bibliography

Works by Henry Miller:

The Air-Conditioned Nightmare. New York: New Directions, 1970.

Aller-Retour New York, Introduction by George Wickes. New York: New Directions, 1991.

Big Sur and the Oranges of Hieronymus Bosch. New York: New Directions, 1957.

Black Spring. New York: Grove Weidenfeld, 1989.

The Books in My Life. New York: New Directions, 1969.

The Colossus of Maroussi. New York: New Directions, 1958.

The Cosmological Eye. New York: New Directions, 1939.

A Devil in Paradise. New York: New Directions, 1993.

Nexus (The Rosy Crucifixion III). New York: Grove Weidenfeld, 1987.

Plexus (The Rosy Crucifixion II). New York: Grove Weidenfeld, 1987.

Quiet Days in Clichy. New York: Grove Weidenfeld, 1987.

Remember to Remember. New York: New Directions, 1961.

Sexus (The Rosy Crufixion I). New York: Grove Weidenfeld, 1987.

Stand Still Like the Hummingbird. New York: New Directions, 1962.

Sunday After the War. New York: New Directions, 1944.

The Time of the Assassins. A Study of Rimbaud. New York: New Directions, 1962.

Tropic of Cancer. New York: Modern Library Edition, 1983.

Tropic of Capricorn. New York: Grove Weidenfeld, 1965.

"What Are You Going to Do About Alf?" Third edition. Beverly Glenn: January 1944.

The Wisdom of the Heart. New York: New Directions, 1960.

Correspondence:

Hargraves, Michael, ed. *Henry Miller's Hamlet Letters.* Santa Barbara: Capra Press, 1988.

MacNiven, Ian S., ed. *The Durrell-Miller Letters, 1935–1980.* New York: New Directions, 1988.

Stuhlmann, Gunther, ed. *A Literate Passion: Letters of Anaïs Nin and Henry Miller, 1932–1953.* San Diego: Harcourt Brace Jovanovich, 1987.